REFORMATION 500

SOURCEBOOK

Anniversary Resources
for Congregations

AUGSBURG FORTRESS

REFORMATION 500 SOURCEBOOK
Anniversary Resources for Congregations

As part of the ELCA's observance of the 500th anniversary of the Reformation, this Sourcebook was shaped by a Congregation Reformation Resources task force, convened jointly by the Office of the Presiding Bishop, ELCA, and Augsburg Fortress. Members of the task force were Linda Witte Henke, Kathryn Kleinhans, Craig Mueller, and Carmelo Santos, with staff participation by H. Karl Reko, Marcus Kunz, Heather Dean, Robert Farlee, and Martin A. Seltz. Gratitude is expressed to Thrivent Financial for support through its Reformation Anniversary Grant Program that assisted in the funding of Congregation Reformation Resources development.

Editor: Robert Farlee
Cover art: Rafael López
Cover design: Laurie Ingram
Interior design: Ivy Palmer Skrade
Publisher: Martin A. Seltz

ISBN 978-1-5064-0637-4

Manufactured in the U.S.A.

1 2 3 4 5 6 7 8 9 10

TABLE OF CONTENTS

Preserve, Support, and Serve

Plan, Explore, and Publicize

WELCOME

Dear brothers and sisters in Christ,

October 31, 2017, marks the 500th anniversary of Martin Luther posting his Ninety-Five Theses on the church door in Wittenberg, Germany—an act that sparked the Lutheran Reformation. I invite you to become involved in the various ways that the Evangelical Lutheran Church in America is observing this anniversary.

Resources such as this *Reformation 500 Sourcebook* represent one important aspect of the ELCA's observance. I encourage you to explore and mine its contents to assist your planning for your local context.

A little more than a year before the anniversary, on **August 10-13, 2016**, we are hosting the **Grace Gathering** in conjunction with the ELCA Churchwide Assembly in New Orleans. This special event gives Grace Gathering attendees and Churchwide Assembly voting members an opportunity to come together in kicking off the 500th anniversary! We are pleased to provide a gratis copy of this Sourcebook to each registrant for the Grace Gathering.

I also invite and encourage you to become involved in the ELCA's ongoing observance of the 500th anniversary of the Reformation into 2017 and beyond by visiting and bookmarking **www.ELCA500.org**, a growing hub of resources, events, and news surrounding preparation for the observance. You also can follow current developments on Facebook at **ELCA Reformation 500**.

Grace and peace to you,

The Rev. Elizabeth A. Eaton
Presiding Bishop
Evangelical Lutheran Church in America

HOW DO WE OBSERVE THE 500TH ANNIVERSARY OF THE REFORMATION?

The first instinct for many will be to throw a big party. Give thanks! Celebrate! And there will be plenty of that as we near the year 2017, five hundred years since Martin Luther posted the Ninety-Five Theses in the city of Wittenberg, Germany.

But there is more to marking this milestone. Luther and a number of his reforming companions were teachers—of university students, of pastors and bishops, of laypeople. So education has a rightful place in our observance. They took part in conversations—with varying success—with Christians of various traditions. So ecumenical connections deserve to be included in our plans. And to be candid, the events of the Reformation era resulted in divisions in the church that continue to this day. Luther and some who have followed his teachings have done and said some hurtful and damaging things. So lament and repentance will also color our observance. These are just a few of the dynamics of this anniversary, which extend to the fields of worship and music, the sciences and cultural studies, social action and public witness, and many more.

The Lutheran church is diverse, and it is decentralized—meaning that no one will be giving congregations a blueprint for how they should observe this anniversary. Those choices will vary, depending on your context. Here is an invitation to form the plans your congregation will make. Through several avenues, the Evangelical Lutheran Church in America and Augsburg Fortress are highlighting a wide range of ideas and possibilities from various sources. We hope the information and resources in this sourcebook encourage you to start planning today. A checklist to help you organize your observance is included in this sourcebook on p. 175.

And remember, this anniversary involves much more than one year. Significant events of the Lutheran branch of the Reformation continued over the decades following, including the Leipzig Debates in 1519, the Diet of Worms in 1521, the publication of the Small Catechism in 1529, and the Augsburg Confession in 1530. How might the observance of five hundred years of Reformation continue in your context in the years ahead? How might taking that longer view give you some breathing room for your observance rather than trying to fit it all into one year or one day?

How will Lutherans observe this anniversary in ways that are forward-looking, outward-directed, and focused on the amazing mercy of God in Jesus Christ? Blessings to you and your congregation as you seek to answer that question in the places where you live and serve.

WHAT'S IN THE REFORMATION 500 SOURCEBOOK, and How Might You Use It?

As the title of this book suggests, you will find within it a wide variety of materials related to the 500th anniversary of the Reformation. None of it will be useful for every situation, but it is wide-ranging enough that all congregations should find ideas to enrich their observances.

Beyond this introductory material, the book is divided into three main sections, plus a list of additional resources and a CD-ROM on the inside back cover that contains materials for easy reproduction and use. In the list below, items with this icon ✪ may be suitable for printing and distribution, and so can be found on the CD-ROM.

Pray, Praise, and Give Thanks

We begin, appropriately, with worship. The actual anniversary of the Ninety-Five Theses is one day, but in many congregations the Reformation anniversary will play a role in worship planning for months, even a full year, in advance—and perhaps beyond, since October 31, 1517, was just the beginning of the Reformation.

Planning Worship for the Reformation 500 Observance Kevin Strickland ✪

The ELCA's director for worship offers suggestions for those who will shape liturgies, whether on a Sunday morning or in a special context. This is a great place to begin your discussions.

Ongoing Reformation: Worship in an Ecumenical Age Craig Mueller ✪

The Reformation brought many gifts to the wider church, but we Lutherans have also gained much from other traditions. Here an ELCA pastor lifts up some examples and provides questions for group discussion.

Alternate Worship Texts for Observances of the Reformation Anniversary ✪

Some of the alternate texts provided in Sundays and Seasons 2017 *are particularly well suited to worship related to the Reformation, and those are reprinted here.*

Worship Helps for Reformation Sunday ✪

Also from Sundays and Seasons 2017 *and its companion volume,* Sundays and Seasons: Preaching 2017, *here are sample prayers of intercession and preaching helps crafted around the Reformation Day propers and those for the Sundays on which Reformation Sunday will fall, Lectionary 31 (2016) and Lectionary 30 (2017).*

Thanksgivings at the Table for the Anniversary of the Reformation Gail Ramshaw

The eleven eucharistic prayers contained in Evangelical Lutheran Worship *are just a beginning. Dr. Ramshaw is a scholar and artist who has worked creatively with eucharistic praying, and here she brings new thanksgivings at the table in two different styles, suitable for Reformation, church anniversaries, and other occasions.*

Hymns for the Anniversary Year

Some hymns are naturals for the Reformation observance. Beyond the obvious, though, what other hymns might be considered, even beyond late October? Here is an annotated list of hymn and song recommendations (how to use, why this hymn) for observing the Reformation anniversary through the year.

The Hymn of the Day as Reformation Inheritance Mark Mummert

We may not often think of the hymn of the day, the central hymn of our worship, as a Lutheran contribution. Here, reprinted from Sundays and Seasons, *a prominent musician invites us to give more thought to this element in which the assembly proclaims God's word.*

Common Prayer / Oración Común: From Conflict to Communion: Lutheran–Catholic Common Commemoration of the Reformation in 2017

This is an order for a prayer service prepared jointly by the Lutheran World Federation and the Vatican. It is the basis for a service to be held in Lund, Sweden, in October 2016. It is here presented in both English and Spanish.

Evening Prayer / Oración de la Tarde

From the Lutheran World Federation publication Koinonia, *this is a simple order for evening prayer. It is printed in English and Spanish, and versions in French and German are also provided on the CD-ROM.*

Midweek Lenten Series Based on Luther's Small Catechism Lynn Bulock

Intended for midweek worship, each week is based on a different section of the catechism. The order is opening dialogue, gathering song, reading, reflection, song, prayer, blessing, sending song. The series is prepared by an ELCA diaconal minister.

The Church's Journey in Art and Song: How to Adapt and Contextualize Scott Weidler

An outline for a festival of song and the arts, based on the one presented at the Worship Jubilee in Atlanta in July 2015; with many suggestions and resources for adapting to different circumstances. The CD-ROM includes plenty of related resources.

Prayers and Blessings Based on Those in Luther's Small Catechism Jennifer Baker-Trinity

At the end of the Small Catechism (see ELW, pp. 1166–67), Luther provided some prayers and blessings. Here an ELCA associate in ministry takes the patterns of the prayers in the Small Catechism and offers new words for different occasions and circumstances.

Read, Mark, and Learn

Education has always been an important facet of the Lutheran community. Here are some ways to enrich our learning about the Reformation and the people and events within it.

Introducing Resources for Children and Adults

In addition to this sourcebook, two other major resources have been developed by Augsburg Fortress to enhance education about the Reformation and Lutherans. This article introduces Papa Luther *(for children) and* Together by Grace *(for adults), and gives some ideas for how they might be used.*

Studies by and for Lutherans and Roman Catholics Kathryn Johnson ⊙

In recent years, three significant books about the continuing Reformation have been written by Roman Catholic and Lutheran teams. Here the ELCA's executive for ecumenical and inter-religious relations presents a comparative guide to those resources, From Conflict to Communion; Declaration on the Way: Church, Ministry, and Eucharist; *and* One Hope: Re-Membering the Body of Christ.

Commemorating 1517 without Dressing Up as Luther with a Hammer Gail Ramshaw ⊙

Beginning with its lighthearted title, a respected ELCA scholar here provides engaging and practical thoughts on observing the anniversary in creative yet authentic ways. This article is based on Dr. Ramshaw's presentation at the 2015 ELCA Worship Jubilee in Atlanta.

The Ninety-Five Theses ⊙

This is the list of propositions for debate that sparked the Reformation, yet some people haven't ever seen what they actually said. Here they are with a brief introduction and information about an excellent study guide.

Martin Luther, the Catechism, and Music Kathryn Kleinhans ⊙

Most people know that Luther sometimes expressed his theology in hymns as a way to communicate with ordinary Christians. In addition to well-known hymns like "A Mighty Fortress" and "Lord, Keep Us Steadfast," he wrote a hymn on each chief part of the Catechism. Professor Kleinhans from Wartburg College offers a study of these five catechism hymns.

Movies about Martin Luther: An Overview

If you want to view a movie to learn more about Luther and the Reformation, what offerings are available, and how do they compare? Here are synopses of some candidates.

A Contemporary Lutheran Approach to Inter-Religious Relations ⊙

ELCA Consultative Panel on Lutheran–Jewish Relations

Martin Luther clearly brought much good not only to the church but to the wider world. Yet it doesn't serve anyone well to overlook his more problematic statements, especially those regarding the Jewish people from later in his life. Asking the provocative question "Why Follow Luther past 2017?" this document suggests a path toward a fair assessment of the reformer for today.

Reformation Timeline ⊙

What happened when in the Reformation, and for context, what else was going on in the world at that time?

"About the Lutherans" Bulletin Inserts ⊙

As a way to help inform congregation members about the Reformation and the Lutheran Church, twelve bulletin inserts on diverse topics have been prepared and are available in PDF format on the CD-ROM.

Preserve, Support, and Serve

Our faith needs always to take active form. Much of this service will not change because of the Reformation anniversary, but here are a few items to spur deeper thought and practical ideas.

Toward a Lutheran Theology for Social and Ecological Justice Carmelo Santos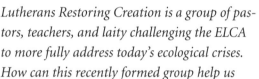

> *Dr. Santos's essay proposes groundings in Lutheran theology for care of creation, working for justice and peace, and serving the neighbor. In what ways can Lutheran theology point us toward a path that leads in the direction of social and ecological justice?*

An Eco-Justice Reformation for 2017 and Beyond David Rhoads

> *Lutherans Restoring Creation is a group of pastors, teachers, and laity challenging the ELCA to more fully address today's ecological crises. How can this recently formed group help us benefit the natural creation?*

Living Out the Small Catechism

> *We think of the catechism as something to study and memorize, but how can it also direct us toward deeds? This article suggests practical ideas based on the structure of the Small Catechism—particularly the Ten Commandments, the Apostles' Creed, and the Lord's Prayer.*

Plan, Explore, and Publicize

Organizing Your Reformation Observance: A Checklist

> *A list of practical ideas for getting your Reformation observance off the ground and into action, sorted by various areas of the congregation's life.*

For Further Exploration

> *This sourcebook is just a beginning—many other resources are available to learn about Luther and the Reformation, to draw in congregational and community members of all ages. Here is a listing of some of those—books, films and other media, and websites.*

Reformation Anniversary Communications Guide

> *The Lutheran Reformation succeeded partly because of the media—specifically, the printing press. Print is still an effective means of communication, but so are other, more recent forms. This article well help you make good use of them and help make your task easier.*

PRAY, PRAISE, AND GIVE THANKS

PLANNING WORSHIP FOR THE REFORMATION 500 OBSERVANCE

As we approach the 500th anniversary of the Reformation, many will be planning worship services for the occasion. As we approach that task, I find Marty Haugen's words to the hymn "Soli Deo Gloria" (ELW 878) to be a helpful perspective:

> All praise for Jesus, best gift divine
> through word and witness, in bread and wine;
> incarnate love song of boundless grace,
> priest, teacher, prophet in time and space,
> your steadfast kindness with human face:
> Soli Deo gloria! Soli Deo gloria!
>
> A billion voices in one great song,
> now soft and gentle, now deep and strong,
> in every culture and style and key,
> from hill and valley, with sky and sea,
> with Christ we praise you eternally:
> Soli Deo gloria! Soli Deo gloria!
> ©1999 GIA Publications, Inc.

Whether your approach to planning worship for this anniversary is one of observation, celebration, commemoration, reconciliation, or a combination of all four, may we remember that we are a church that isn't reformed, but reforming. May we remember that we are a church that does not hold a monopoly on all of the answers of the Christian faith. May we remember, and even allow, moments of lament for the history of division that has occurred and harmful words that have been used in God's name toward our sisters and brothers. May we remember that we are a church that is part of a much larger body—the body of Christ.

In crafting these liturgies, whether it is for a Sunday morning service, a multicongregational service, or an ecumenical service, how do we uplift the *means of grace* and point people to Jesus as that "best gift divine"? We do this by pointing people to word and water, bread and wine, song and prayer.

Moving to more specific things to keep in mind in preparing worship, keep your eyes open for ways to balance the ordo (gathering/word/meal/sending) within a special service:
- The prayers of intercession, at their best, are always crafted by someone locally for the particular context. Many different Reformation themes can be woven into carefully prepared prayers.

- The gathering and sending segments are the most flexible moments in the holy communion liturgy. These are wonderful moments to envision language specific to the Reformation commemoration, gathering God's people together in a spirit of reconciliation and not Lutheran triumphalism, being sent out into God's world as ambassadors of love and unity.
- Less is more. It is important to keep in mind that the fourfold pattern of the ordo can easily be used regardless of the special service, but everything does not have to be included within each part.

What readings will you use? Lutherans should be able to commemorate the Reformation with any words of scripture. However, most of us use the lectionary commended by the ELCA and included in our two most recent books of worship, the Revised Common Lectionary. Within that listing, the two primary choices for a service on Sunday, October 29, 2017, are Reformation Day (*ELW*, p. 58) or Lectionary 30 A (*ELW*, p. 51). The Reformation Day selections have the advantage of being chosen specifically for a celebration such as this. But the Lectionary 30 option has at least two advantages:

- These are the readings we share with both the Roman Catholic Church, our partners in reconciliation and continuing reformation, and many of our siblings from the Reformation, such as the Episcopal, Methodist, and Presbyterian churches.
- The gospel, with its call to "love the Lord your God" and "love your neighbor as yourself," would provide a strong basis for preaching. And of course you can still use the prayer of the day for Reformation and incorporate Reformation themes throughout the worship.

This book contains helpful thoughts to keep in mind in planning music, so here I will just suggest that appropriate hymns and songs might well include those from Luther's time but should not be limited to those. The music chosen should also pick up on the themes of the church, which is ever-reforming (new and looking toward the future). It is important to show that we are a church that is not made up of just Germans and Scandinavians, but of a wide and diverse people. Therefore, selecting and singing (perhaps teaching new) songs from Lutherans and other Christians from around the world will do well to show this diversity.

Other important questions to keep in mind:

- How are children, youth, and young adults being included, both as leaders and participants, as these liturgies are being planned?
- How is diversity and inclusivity being represented both in your planning and within the liturgies themselves? What does that look like in your congregation or community?
- Have you thought of including ecumenical partners as part of these special services? If so, it is important to provide hospitality and collegial partnerships within the language used in the liturgy and leadership roles.

Activist Mary Harris "Mother" Jones once said, "Reformation, like education, is a journey, not a destination." We Christians, who live out our faith lives as Lutherans, remember the Reformation, but do so knowing that it is still occurring. If we view the Reformation and what it means to be a reforming people of faith, as journeys, not destinations, then we have to be honest that, along the way, discomfort and challenges will accompany joy.

The journey we travel as reforming people is one that begins in the waters of our baptism, when we are immersed into a lifelong walk with God and God's people—the church. What does it mean to be a member of this church? I think it means what it has always meant as a church of reformation-minded people; we are a church that is centered on the means of grace, one that deeply cares for the needs of our neighbors and one serving as the visible gospel to the world. As Presiding Bishop Elizabeth Eaton has said, "We are not called to be the church of the past nor the church of some distant future, but to be the church right now. For whatever reason, we are the ones God is using at this time in this messiness. We are not going to get it right all of the time. We are broken and sinful creatures, but we are also redeemed creatures. In baptism we have already died the only death that really matters. Can we start to live like we believe that?"

Living like we believe this to be true means we live as baptized children of God who lead lives filled with great joy and great hope. Even in the moments of life when all seems lost, we are found by God's prodigal, lavish love for each of us and for all of us. The lavish love pours over us, in us, and through us so that we may be visible, tangible signs of God's great reformation journey to the entire world.

To live this love completely and to truly believe that reformation did not happen just in the past, we must live knowing that we are a reforming people and reformation is still happening. This can be accomplished by how we live and how we work. This can be realized by how we pray and how we act. This can be achieved by how we treat our neighbors and love our enemies.

This can be done in how we have dialogue and conversations with people who offer differing views from our own. This can be lived out each and every time we gather around the word proclaimed, the bath, and the meal—in the gathered assembly in worship.

May this resource provide for you great tools in your planning! Blessings on the journey!

Kevin L. Strickland

ONGOING REFORMATION
Worship in an Ecumenical Age

REFORMATION REFORMS

Worship is the primary gathering of the church. As we celebrate the 500th anniversary of the Reformation, a logical starting place is to name a number of liturgical reforms that date back to that period:

- Mass (word and sacrament) in the vernacular
- Communion in both kinds (bread and wine)
- Centrality of scripture
- Emphasis on congregational singing
- Two sacraments (baptism and eucharist)
- Removal of sacrificial language in the canon of the Mass (what we call the eucharistic prayer)
- Texts in the hands of worshipers (advent of the printing press)
- Emphasis on preaching (law and gospel)
- The presence of Christ in the eucharist described as real presence, "in, with, and under," rather than either transubstantiation or mere symbolic presence
- Worship as nourishment for laity living their baptismal vocation in the world

VATICAN II REFORMS

For over four centuries, worship in Lutheran and Roman Catholic churches would have looked significantly different. Yet Vatican II (1962–65) brought these reforms to Roman Catholic liturgy:

- Mass in the vernacular
- Communion in both kinds (in principle, though not always in practice)
- Scripture and preaching given new emphasis
- Emphasis on congregational song
- Liturgy defined as the full, active, and conscious participation of all worshipers
- Concelebration of the eucharist (by multiple priests) deemphasized
- Increased use of "real presence" to describe the presence of Christ in the eucharist and in the assembled body of Christ
- Laity take on expanded roles in the liturgy

ECUMENICAL CONSENSUS

In a ripple effect, the reforms of Vatican II brought significant changes in Protestant worship. Beginning in the mid-1960s, the fruits of Vatican II not only affected Lutheran worship reforms but also brought about a growing ecumenical consensus regarding the central movements, texts, actions, and theology of liturgy.

For Lutherans, the unity and continuity of the church through the ages is a guiding principle. The Lutheran Confessions set our liturgical life within the mainstream of Christian worship: "We do not abolish the Mass but religiously keep and defend it. . . . We keep traditional liturgical forms" (*Apology to the Augsburg Confession*, 24).

In the decades that followed Vatican II, an ecumenical approach to worship brought Christian denominations together. What many saw as innovative worship reforms—such as the greeting of peace shared by the congregation—were actually a restoration of practices from the early centuries of the church. In addition, common liturgical texts and a three-year lectionary—held in common with Roman Catholics—began appearing in the worship books of Lutherans, Episcopalians, Presbyterians, Methodists, and many others.

CATHOLIC LUTHERANS

A majority of ELCA Lutheran congregations now celebrate weekly eucharist, and the alb and, sometimes, the chasuble have become the normative vestments. Many Lutherans are more comfortable with an array of bodily gestures: the *orans* position for prayer, bowing, kneeling, making the sign of the cross, to name a few. Add ashes, anointing with oil, processions, and the like. Things many Lutherans would have resisted and called "Catholic" fifty years ago are now common in many of our congregations.

There has also been a gradual movement away from anti-catholic attitudes in which Lutherans were defined over and against Roman Catholicism to one in which people freely admit that Lutherans are very close to the Roman Church, at least in our core liturgical practices, theology, and interpretation of scripture. Some Lutherans joke that we are "Catholic lite." Perhaps it would be better to say that we both are part of the stream of Western Christianity and that we hold a vast majority of our worship practices in common with Roman Catholics. Maybe it was always so. Martin Luther retained much of the liturgical tradition of his day. Yet the reforms of Vatican II—especially worship in the vernacular—made people notice that we were more similar than different.

Take the word *catholic*. Some of us remember the uproar when Lutherans started restoring the phrase "I believe in the one holy catholic and apostolic church" in the creeds of *Lutheran Book of Worship* (1978). *Catholic* was the accurate, historic word, but it was hard for some Lutherans to swallow. That small change led to one of the preeminent pastoral teaching moments of the 1970s: small *c catholic* meant "universal," not the Roman Catholic Church.

ECUMENICAL REFORMS SINCE VATICAN II

Whether we call them catholic practices or within an ecumenical consensus, consider these reforms in the liturgy from the past several decades:
- Vestments: albs and chasubles
- Centrality of baptism in faith and life
- Weekly eucharist

- Recovery of Lent as a season for baptismal preparation and renewal
- Recovery of the Three Days, including the Vigil of Easter
- Free-standing table/altar
- Ecumenical three-year lectionary
- Fuller use of sacramental signs (generous use of water; real bread for communion)
- Restoration of thanksgiving prayers in baptismal and eucharistic rites
- Anointing with oil (baptism, healing)
- Expanded use of processions (gospel and offertory processions)

As we celebrate the Reformation in 2017, we see a striking resemblance in the rites of the major branches of Western Christianity—a reason to celebrate our oneness in baptism even as we long for greater unity at the Lord's table.

To use the above material in a forum or discussion, have participants read the short essay or work through the material using these questions:

1. What aspects of Lutheran worship date back to Reformation reforms?

2. Name reforms in Roman Catholic worship as a result of Vatican II.

3. When you visit churches of other denominations (Roman Catholic and Protestant), what similarities and differences do you notice with Lutheran worship?

4. What does it mean that Lutherans are catholic?

5. Discuss the ecumenical consensus regarding worship reform and some changes in Lutheran worship during the past four decades.

6. Lutherans have always emphasized a certain freedom in regard to worship practices. What are the central things we have in common with each other and those of other denominations?

Craig Mueller

ALTERNATE WORSHIP TEXTS FOR OBSERVANCES OF THE REFORMATION ANNIVERSARY

Note: These texts are also provided in *Sundays and Seasons 2017*, on page 252.

CONFESSION AND FORGIVENESS

All may make the sign of the cross, the sign marked at baptism, as the presiding minister begins.

Blessed be the + holy Trinity,
the one who fashions us,
the one who heals us,
the one who reforms us again and again.
Amen.

Let us confess our sin, calling for God's transforming power.

Silence for reflection and self-examination.

Source of all life,
we confess that we have not allowed
your grace to set us free.
We fear that we are not good enough.
We hear your word of love freely given to us,
yet we expect others to earn it.
We turn the church inward,
rather than moving it outward.
Forgive us. Stir us.
Reform us to be a church powered by love,
willing to speak for what is right,
act for what is just,
and seek the healing of your whole creation. Amen.

God hears our cry and sends the Spirit to change us
and to empower our lives in the world.
Our sins are forgiven,
+ God's love is unconditional,
and we are raised up as God's people who will always be made new,
in the name of Jesus Christ.
Amen.

OFFERING PRAYER

God of life,
you give us these gifts of the earth,
these resources of our life and our labor.
Take them, offered in great thanksgiving,
and use them to set a table that will heal the whole creation;
through Jesus Christ, our Savior and Light.
Amen.

INVITATION TO COMMUNION

Speak to us, O Lord, in the breaking of the bread,
and make us one with you.

PRAYER AFTER COMMUNION

Holy and compassionate God,
in bread and wine you give us gifts
that form us to be humble and courageous.
May your words come to life
in our serving and in our witness,
that we might speak a living voice
of healing and justice to all the world,
through Jesus Christ, our rock and our redeemer.
Amen.

BLESSING

God, creator of all things, speaking reformation into being;
Jesus Christ, savior of the world, raising the dead;
Holy Spirit, living voice, calling and enlightening the church:
Almighty God, Father, + Son, and Holy Spirit,
bless you now and forever.
Amen.

DISMISSAL

Go in peace. Sound the good news.
Thanks be to God.

WORSHIP HELPS FOR REFORMATION SUNDAY

The following materials are reprinted from Sundays and Seasons 2016 (Year C) and 2017 (Year A), and Sundays and Seasons: Preaching 2016 and 2017. Since the day may be observed using either the lectionary propers assigned for the date or those for Reformation Day, both are provided.

October 30, 2016
Lectionary 31 C

SAMPLE PRAYERS OF INTERCESSION
The prayers are prepared locally for each occasion. The following examples may be adapted or used as appropriate.

Set free by the truth of God's gracious love, we pray for the church, the world, and all of God's good creation.
A brief silence.
Continue to reform your church, O God. Unite it in mission. Teach it to grow in service. Send it to those who do not yet know your love. Hear us, O God.
Your mercy is great.
Call us to repent our destructive actions toward your beautiful creation. Help us to leave our children and grandchildren a world in which to live and thrive. Hear us, O God.
Your mercy is great.
Call the nations to account, O God. Show leaders and governments the way to peace. Awaken in us a desire for the well-being of all people, both our friends and our enemies. Hear us, O God.
Your mercy is great.
Show your mercy to all those who call on you in times of trouble. Provide for the poor, heal the sick, and comfort the grieving. Especially we pray for. . . . Hear us, O God.
Your mercy is great.
Teach us to welcome the stranger as Christ himself. Prepare us to receive newcomers and visitors in this assembly with true hospitality and gracious care. Hear us, O God.
Your mercy is great.
Here other intercessions may be offered.
We give thanks for all the faithful witnesses and renewers of the church who have gone before us (*especially*) and who now enjoy eternal life with you. Hear us, O God.
Your mercy is great.

Into your hands, faithful God, we place ourselves and our prayers, spoken and unspoken, trusting in your mercy; through Jesus Christ, our Savior.
Amen.

PREACHING IDEAS
From a Scholar

The first reading (complementary series) is one of the finest summaries of prophetic theology in all of the Bible. Do you, preacher, have the courage to open your sermon with, "Hear the word of the LORD, you sodomites"? How about, speaking God's words, "Even though you make many prayers, I will not listen" (Isa. 1:15)?

One way to approach this text, as God's continuing word of scripture for the church today, is as a critique of divinely ordained liturgy that is not enlivened by ethics—in other words, worship without right living. Keep in mind that all the liturgical acts criticized by Isaiah are commanded by God in the Torah. One could paraphrase the text as follows (imagine this in your own parish setting): "Listen to the word of God, you who live in Sodom and Gomorrah! What to me is the multitude of your eucharists? I have had enough of baptisms and confirmations. Don't come trampling down the aisle of the church; who asked you to be here? Sunday worship and Advent services make me sick: I cannot endure your worship with your sinful living. Christmas Eve and Christmas Day weary me; so don't pray anymore, because I have stopped listening."

There is another way to read this passage. From the beginning of the prophets to their end is the theme that God desires a life of love and faithful living, not sacrifices at the temple in Jerusalem (see, for example, Hos. 6:6). Jesus wept over the temple and foretold its downfall, as had prophets before him. We, the church, are the new temple, the new Jerusalem. We must believe and proclaim this without anti-Semitism or supersessionism, but boldly.

"For I must stay at your house today" (Luke 19:5). Zacchaeus's house is the new house of God, temple of Jerusalem. He has, to borrow an image from the semicontinuous first reading, made the transition from the proud whose spirit is not right, to the righteous who live by faith (Hab. 2:4). It is the house of a sinner who repents. And when salvation comes to this house, "he too is a son of Abraham" (Luke 19:9). The preacher can relate this to the Reformation text (John 8:31-36), where some in the audience claim to be children of Abraham and therefore slaves to nothing, including sin.

The words of the psalm (complementary) are some of the most profound in the Bible. When the sinners/worshipers refused to confess their sin, they wasted away. But upon confession, their sins were flushed away (Ps. 32:5-6). The liturgy is a time in Zacchaeus's house.

Lamontte M. Luker

From a Preacher

My father pastored a small, struggling church in the South Bronx of New York City in the late 1960s and early '70s. We have stories of great tragedy, profound courage, and disarming hilarity from that time in my family's life. As the years pass, I wonder if certain stories really happened at our church or if they came from my father's colleagues. One iconic story, whether it happened to us or at another nearby parish, speaks with power on this day.

A congregation member regularly went to the surrounding tenement buildings to visit the poor. A poor man himself, he would knock on the door, be welcomed inside, and find a place to sit, which sometimes meant squatting on a dirt floor or perching on an old milk crate. After he found his seat, he would ask for a glass of water—a small yet provocative act.

The poverty in the South Bronx was almost unspeakable, but even the poorest of the poor had a faucet and a cup. This man—a representative of the congregation sent to show mercy and provide support—asked for a glass of water to remind his hosts of their power, however humble: *I have come not only to serve you. I have come to likewise be served, and to encourage empowerment and justice for us both.*

Serving up the confounding Christian paradox of mercy and justice is your task as a preacher today. The question of how to nurture a soft and loving heart while simultaneously stoking the flames of justice has perplexed everyone from Thich Nhat Hanh to Mohandas Gandhi to Dorothy Day to Martin Luther King Jr.

The lectionary provides you with a full selection from a challenging menu. It leads off with the fervency of Isaiah's frustration and anger at the lack of justice (echoed in the semicontinuous selection from Habakkuk), switches to the relief and joy of living in God's mercy in Psalm 32, encourages "steadfastness and faith during all your persecutions and the afflictions that you are enduring" in Paul's second letter to the Thessalonians, and finally the gospel from Luke combines these earlier themes and culminates in the offense—to the people in the crowd—of Jesus' acknowledgment of Zacchaeus in the tree and, after the tax collector welcomes him, that salvation has come to Zacchaeus and his house.

Zacchaeus may have represented a frightening and traitorous reminder of the Roman occupation to any bystander at the scene: he and his ilk often collected exorbitant taxes on behalf of the empire. Zacchaeus was at worst an enemy collaborator and at best a social pariah. His despised vocation and corresponding self-enrichment cried out for justice. Shockingly, Jesus' response was to fully see and lovingly provoke Zacchaeus rather than ignore or condemn him. Jesus engaged Zacchaeus with a challenge of kindness, encouraging and celebrating his process of repentance.

"Let us argue it out," thunders the LORD in Isaiah. Indeed: let us argue out the paradox of a need for justice with the assurance of grace, assigning Jesus' approach to Zacchaeus a favored seat at the negotiations. As lead negotiator, from either the pulpit or your chosen place of proclamation, you might argue for the Zacchaeus in all of us, risking collective identification with what seems to have been to Jesus' followers and listeners the least sympathetic character in the gospel.

Your congregation is not a group of innocent bystanders, watching dispassionately as an undeserving scapegoat struggles piteously up a tree. No, we are all Zacchaeus-like in damnable ways simply by nature of claiming citizenship in *this* empire. Whether tacitly or through willful ignorance, we prop up systems of rampant individualism, greed, exclusion, and militarism. We turn our heads the other way when confronted with what it would take to achieve justice. We daily collect the wages of sin for all those things and more.

But rather than shame or blame your people—hypocritically implicating yourself in the process—why not allow your sisters and brothers to be seen, challenged, and encouraged with the same ringmaster spirit in which Jesus sees, challenges, and encourages Zacchaeus?

Your people know the frustrated, even anguished, sensation of not easily comprehending or addressing large-scale problems. They are saturated by a daily, demonic message of commodified personhood. They trash their possessions, apps, relationships, and technologies as they lose their luster, only to begin another mad scramble for the next existential salve through drugs, alcohol, affairs, or digital isolation. If they are sitting in your congregation today, they likely hunger with great urgency, as Zacchaeus did. They hunger to be fully seen, fully known, and mercifully encouraged toward repentance and grace.

They, like those poor citizens of the South Bronx, know they have an inherent self-worth, a calling, and a responsibility—no matter their brokenness and feelings of impotency. Hand over Jesus' challenge and assurance as he did to Zacchaeus: *I have come not only to serve you. I have come to likewise be served, and to encourage empowerment and justice for us both.* The beloved host of forgiven sinners in front of you is struggling up the tree of their tangled, modern lives to receive the same mystery of mercy and justice. It is the heart of Jesus' message to Zacchaeus, to be negotiated with your people through joyful provocation on a day when they and our broken world desperately need it.

Daniel Ruen

MAKING CONNECTIONS

- The sharing of the peace is meant to restore relationships and practice deep reconciliation, as well as offer a greeting of peace and joy. This may be a day to remind your people of its full power. The eucharist is a not only a primary sacrament of God's grace; God's yearning for justice is represented in all being welcome to the table regardless of economic status, ethnicity, gender identity, sexual orientation, age, disability, or politics.

- Your congregation has Halloween somewhere in their heads and hearts today. Even the singles without children and elders have powerful connections to knocking on someone's door or being the person who opens that door. Second only to Christmas in overall profitability, Halloween absolutely envelops American culture in October. The ancient Celtic festival of Samhain originally featured food and drink left outside one's front door to fool wandering demons who might be masquerading as animals. When costumes were adorned, they were probably made of animal hides, meant to blend in with other evil spirits. While there was a positive side to Samhain in people's desire to communicate or otherwise somehow connect with one's beloved ancestors (similar to *El Dia de los Muertos*—the Day of the Dead—as practiced in Mexico, Central America, and South America), it is striking to me that the ancient emphasis for what became our modern-day Halloween activities was in keeping things *out*, not letting them *in*. Jesus demands to be let in, even as we too often try to keep out the responsibilities of justice and implications of God's mercy in our lives.

- After Samhain was co-opted by Christianity after the eighth century, a dimension of economic justice entered the picture. Processions of the poor would go down the streets and beg for "soul cakes"—tasty treats with a cross inscribed on them—and if received, they would promise to say special prayers for that household's departed loved ones. Their public processions were an indicator of their power and need, yet they likewise offered a message of mercy through prayer in exchange for food. In some cases, depending on time period and place, there may have been a threat implied by the lower classes if wealthier households did not provide treats. The "trick" was mischief that sometimes devolved to property damage or other acts of confrontation.

- For children, it might be an engaging exercise to put Jesus in the position of a trick-or-treater at the door of Zacchaeus. What is Jesus asking of Zacchaeus, if not candy or other treats? What does Zacchaeus offer to "give" Jesus? What is it like for the children to dress up and be out among their neighbors and other strangers on this one night of every year? How might you make a connection to Jesus' life and ministry and children's ability—or not—to feel free to provocatively engage neighbors and strangers at their doorsteps?

Reformation Sunday 2016

SAMPLE PRAYERS OF INTERCESSION

The prayers are prepared locally for each occasion. The following examples may be adapted or used as appropriate.

Set free by the truth of God's gracious love, we pray for the church, the world, and all of God's good creation.

A brief silence.

Righteous God, write your law on our hearts. Unite your church. Let your word spread throughout the earth. Hear us, O God.

Your mercy is great.

Earth-maker, show your power and goodness in the mountains, the depths of the sea, the rivers, and all of your creation. Teach us how to care for our earthly home. Hear us, O God.

Your mercy is great.

Source of hope, you make wars to cease in all the world. Visit places devastated by war and conflict (*especially*). Break the bow, shatter the spear, and bring your perfect peace. Hear us, O God.

Your mercy is great.

God our refuge and strength, you are a very present help in trouble. Comfort those who are sick or in pain, the lonely and grieving, those without a home or meaningful work. Especially we pray for. . . . Hear us, O God.

Your mercy is great.

Faithful God, call this assembly to remember the everlasting covenant you have made with us. Shape us to live in the freedom Christ gives us and to welcome others into this way of life. Hear us, O God.

Your mercy is great.

Here other intercessions may be offered.

God our stronghold, the saints from every age gather around your throne. Help us to wait with patience and joy until that day when we too see you face to face. Hear us, O God.

Your mercy is great.

Into your hands, faithful God, we place ourselves and our prayers, spoken and unspoken, trusting in your mercy; through Jesus Christ, our Savior.

Amen.

PREACHING IDEAS

From a Scholar

The first reading is one of the clearest statements of the gospel in the entire Bible. Christians must note that it is written in the Old Covenant (Testament) and interpret it in a uniquely Christian way while remembering that it remains a passage in the Jewish Bible. That being said, the Christian Bible concludes with the New Covenant (Testament), which serves for us as the interpretive key to and the fulfillment of the Old.

The First Covenant was/is based on the written law, the Torah. It was/is sealed by a physical sign, circumcision. It is summarized in Deuteronomy 6:1-5, where the voice of Moses speaks: "This is the commandment—the statutes and the ordinances—that the LORD your God charged me to teach you to observe. . . . You shall love the LORD your God with all your heart, and with all your soul, and with all your might." The experience of the prophets Amos, Hosea, Micah, and Isaiah was largely that this covenant had not "worked." The new insight of Jeremiah is that the fundamental problem is not that people do not *want* to do Torah, but that they are inherently *unable* to do it. So God must step in with a miracle and write the Torah on human hearts, make it internal to the human spirit so that the human being is enabled to do Torah and that it is so much a part of their new nature that they need not even teach it—it is obvious to one whose heart has been changed. Deuteronomy 30:6, written probably about the same time as Jeremiah and under his influence, calls this miracle a cardiac circumcision: "The LORD your God will circumcise your heart and the heart of your descendants, so that you will [be able to] love the LORD your God with all your heart and with all your soul." Ezekiel uses baptismal language to describe this miracle as an infusion, into our natural human hard and stony hearts, of God's Holy Spirit, who will "make you follow my statutes and be careful to observe my ordinances" (36:25-27).

Thus Paul can write that this gospel truth which he expounds so eloquently in the second reading "is attested by the [Torah] and the prophets" (Rom. 3:21). To "know the LORD" (Jer. 31:34) is to "know the truth," Jesus, who makes us free from sin (John 8:31, 34-36).

Lamontte M. Luker

From a Preacher

On this day, reform and tradition collide, change and stasis clash, and celebration and humility compete for our attention. The wise preacher is attentive to how our congregations fear and desire both sides of this Lutheran paradox.

"The truth will set you free!" proclaims Jesus. And some modern-day Lutherans say, "We have never been slaves to anyone!" Some in our congregations have the understanding that our Lutheran tradition has already totally freed us, and we no longer have a need for reform, for freedom, for evaluation of how we have lived out our covenant with God. For some of our listeners, "freedom" and "always reforming" sound like change—change that is unnecessary, as we have always been free. In fact, for some, talk of a new covenant is terrifying.

Others will be sitting in our pews longing for change. Perhaps the very Lutheran tradition we're celebrating has been feeling stuffy, history carries oppressive meanings, and they long for the freedom and reform these texts advocate.

Perhaps we recognize both positions in tension in our congregations, in the people sitting in our pews, and in our very selves.

We're also likely to notice a divide in our congregation's knowledge of Lutheran theology and tradition. As much as we desire that Reformation Sunday will be something other than Lutheran Pride Day, for some of our congregations it will be exactly that. Other worshipers will be completely unaware of the history of the Reformation or how we differ from other Protestant traditions. Some of us will need to do at least a little bit of teaching about what Reformation Sunday is (and some of our congregations will benefit from corrections of previous teaching). We need to resist the temptation to pretend we still live in the sixteenth century. We share our reliance on grace with Roman Catholics, Orthodox believers, and Protestants of all stripes. In all those churches, including our own, many pay lip service to such teachings but inwardly put their—our—trust in earning and paying our way into heaven. At the center of our sermons is not Luther, but Jesus.

One possible way to hold Christ central as we teach core ideas about Reformation is to stay focused on the text, "We hold that a person is justified by faith apart from works prescribed by the law" (Rom. 3:28). The story of how Martin Luther came to a rediscovery of and utter reliance on this grace can illustrate its astounding power and beauty, as can the lived experience of the preacher, our own stories of how we have been changed by grace. The central point is God's gracious and saving action in Jesus Christ; our Lutheran tradition is secondary, one reaction to this miracle.

As we celebrate and teach the heart of our faith, that we are freed by faith in Christ, we may need a reminder that we Lutherans believe the church must always be reforming, because we always need reformation.

What is the law that your congregation needs to hear? Where are the places we are still slave to sin and need the freedom of Christ's truth? Perhaps we can lift up the places where the Lutheran Church has failed to live up to our gospel inheritance. Maybe we talk about how we humans resist having God's law written on our hearts. Surely we should preach about our continuing desire to justify ourselves before God, including our self-congratulation on getting our theology right, on being Lutherans.

As the preacher navigates these waters, we may begin to feel that we are in the midst of Psalm 46, with the earth trembling and the mountains shaking. Just as in the psalm we are taught not to fear, for God holds steady, for those of us who are Lutherans, the gospel provides us with a solid foundation in grace.

God's gracious action in Jesus Christ is the rock upon which we stand, as Lutherans, as Christians, and as people. As we celebrate Lutheran tradition, we stand upon grace; as we fear change, we trust God's grace; as we long for reform, we base it upon God's grace; as we learn about Lutheran tradition, we do it to better understand grace, so that when we preach, we preach grace.

No matter what the setting, the good Lutheran preacher will use the celebration of the Reformation, our congregation's various responses to our tradition, and the texts of the day to preach Jesus, crucified and risen, as we do every day of the church year.

Lura Groen

MAKING CONNECTIONS

- Today more than most days, the way we shape the liturgy will inform how we approach the preaching task. If the congregation insists on the nineteenth- and twentieth-century habit of making this a day to celebrate Lutheran exceptionalism, that kind of pride and anti-ecumenical attitude may need to be addressed in the sermon. Of course it isn't wrong to be grateful for Luther's insights and to hold them up as a centerpiece of our denomination's inheritance. But as noted above, it has to be Christ we lift up, not Luther or Lutheranism. (Next year's observance of the 500th anniversary of the Reformation may, of course, be even more of a challenge in that regard!)

- Because of ecumenical advances in the last century, this would be a good day to lift up explicitly in the intercessory prayers other denominations, giving thanks for the insights and ministry of the Roman Catholic Church as well as the spiritual descendants of Calvin and Zwingli.

- In a time with children, if they are old enough, you might ask, "Why do your parents love you?" You may get some shrugs, some answers like, "Because I help around the house." Finally, tell them that their parents love them because they can't help themselves. They will always love their children. And it is the same with God, who will always love us, no matter what. We can do good things because we love God, but they won't affect God's love for us—God's love is always there.

October 29, 2017

Lectionary 30 A

SAMPLE PRAYERS OF INTERCESSION

The prayers are prepared locally for each occasion. The following examples may be adapted or used as appropriate.

Open to the gifts of the Holy Spirit, we pray for the church, the world, and all of God's creation.
A brief silence.

Holy God, grant courage to your church. In all things and among all people of faith, prosper our Lord's call to love and serve in strength and humility. Hear us, O God.
Your mercy is great.

Holy Creator, protect this world so lovingly made. Align our stewardship with yours so that plants offer shelter and nourishment, water sources sustain life, habitats thrive, and all creation flourishes as you intend. Hear us, O God.
Your mercy is great.

Sovereign God, bring justice to the nations. Turn enemies from vengeance and warfare, direct leaders in fair and honest governance, and equip citizens to seek the needs of their neighbors. Hear us, O God.
Your mercy is great.

Holy Provider, you care for all your children. Heal those in need: the sick and their caregivers (*especially*), victims of family strife, and any who grieve this day. Hear us, O God.
Your mercy is great.

Gracious God, you bless this congregation and community. Reveal your servant love through our ministries, that our work on behalf of our neighbors bears fruit that endures. Hear us, O God.
Your mercy is great.

Here other intercessions may be offered.

We give you thanks, Holy One, for those who served you in this earthly life (*especially*). Renew our hope until that day when all are nourished by your tree of life. Hear us, O God.
Your mercy is great.
Into your hands, gracious God, we commend all for whom we pray, trusting the power of Christ and the gifts of the Spirit.
Amen.

PREACHING IDEAS
From a Scholar

This Sunday's texts depict the law as embodied love. Under pressure from the religious professionals, Jesus responds in Matthew 22 to a question that is meant as a challenge: "Teacher, which commandment in the law is the greatest?" Jesus points immediately to part of the Shema, the central scripture of Judaism, which reads, "You shall love the Lord your God with all your heart, and with all your soul, and with all your might" (Deut. 6:5). The Shema insists that the law is centered in God's identity and, therefore, in love. It is centered in the love of God and, by natural extension, in the love of neighbor. The preacher today has to question, "What has happened with the law that it can seem astonishing today to think of love as its definitive characteristic?"

The Leviticus text offers ten "you shalls." Law seems readily present here. However, listening to the bookends and the center, the chiasm is clear. It starts out, "You shall be holy, for *I the Lord your God am* holy." In the middle of the text, it is confirmed, "*I am the Lord*." The pericope ends with, "you shall love your neighbor as yourself: *I am the Lord*."

God is holy; God's holiness is the beginning, end, and middle of why, how, and for what we are holy. God's holiness leads to our love of our neighbors and to all the "you shalls" in between. God's holiness is the reason we are just, the reason we actively and incessantly pursue relationship with the poor, the reason we bear true witness to our neighbors. God is our God; therefore, we show the law of love in ways resonant with God's actions on behalf of others.

First Thessalonians 2 talks about finding courage in God to share the gospel. This text determinedly asserts that sharing the gospel is not just a mental act but is an embodied act. Paul compares apostles sharing the gospel to a nurse gently caring for her children. Paul says we not only share the gospel in this way; we share ourselves in this way. What are the most congruent ways to embody the law, which is love, and to embody the gospel, which resounds with the life of our crucified and coming Lord?

Jan Rippentrop

From a Preacher

Though not assigned as readings for the Reformation festival, the readings for Lectionary 30 resonate deeply with Reformation themes. Jesus finds himself in a controversy with the religious establishment over interpretation and application of scripture, one that centers upon his messianic identity. Paul confronts opposition to the gospel within a community he knows and loves. While Leviticus speaks of neighbor love, Deuteronomy depicts Moses' death in full view of the promised land and in full knowledge that he won't see it. Contextualized within the Reformation story, these texts can provide fresh perspective on the vitality of the Reformation in present contexts.

In the Gospel of Matthew, two types of characters dare to test Jesus: Satan and the Pharisees. In both situations, the test originates with persons once close to God who now fail to see the presence of God before them. Though Jesus lives as the fulfillment of the law, the religious elite seek to trap him in a semantic argument about the Torah. Instead, Jesus confounds his testers as he quotes the Shema alongside the words of neighbor love in Leviticus. This juxtaposition suggests that love of God leads to love of neighbor, and love of neighbor reveals love of God. As interdependent equals, these commands sum up the law.

This will effectively preach, especially at this time of year. Reformation Sunday reminds us not only of the need for constant reformation in the life of faith but of the proliferation of denominationalism, the fracturing of the body of Christ. Our malformed pursuit of God separates us from our neighbors, our sisters and brothers, the other images of God in the world. This Halloween, children and adults alike will dress as someone else, some out of the simple joy of the holiday, but many others out of a desire to be someone, anyone, else. Further, the popularity of costumes that objectify the body, especially those of women, sensualizes a holiday that once commemorated the faithful departed. Our lust for neighbors and commodification of our bodies distance us from the God who formed us in our mother's womb, who knows the number of hairs upon our heads. We too test God.

Yet when we hold these commandments in tension, we may find transformation. We may find ourselves reformed and reforming. Though denominations seem the norm until Jesus brings a new heaven and earth to fruition, we may come to see the light of God reflected through the one prism of the church, with multiform images offering us unique views into the heart of God and the trajectory of God's community. Though we, like Paul, see opposition to the gospel and to the work of Jesus in our lives, we may find apostles, faithful despite their own flaws, who guide us into renewed communion with God. Imperfect characters like Moses and Luther arise along with present-day saints to help to bring repentance and reformation into our God-given identity. As sinners justified by the grace of God, we see these exemplars guiding us into lives where we too admit our faults as we pursue the kind of life God has in store for us.

Today's gospel also includes Jesus' response to the test, a request for the Pharisees to interpret Psalm 110:1, where David refers to the messiah as "Lord." Since Israel expected a descendant of David to appear as Messiah, and since Hebrew descendants were culturally considered subordinates to parents and ancestors, the question confounds the Pharisees. For modern readers, as those who confess Jesus as God incarnate, the question itself may seem absurd, and the Pharisees' ignorance even more so. Yet, from this posture, we may also admit our own limitations. The cultural blindness and social location of the Pharisees prevented them from seeing the fullness of God before them, the son of David who lives as his Lord. What assumptions do we make that block our vision from the work of God? How does our location in space and time shape us to ignore the work of God among us? We too find ourselves stumped by the presence of God in our midst.

Within this tension, the greatest commandments seem most appropriate because we experience an example of what that looks like in and through Jesus. As the Son of God, Jesus completely loves the Father with heart, soul, and mind, seen in his embrace of imperfect humanity alongside the perfect divinity of God. In this human form, Jesus echoes the Levitical commands and becomes the perfect neighbor, the one who consistently loves neighbors as himself, and often even more than himself. In Matthew's narrative, Jesus will soon refuse to harbor hate or vengeance despite the unjust judgment that leads to his ridicule and death. Jesus is the sign-act of the greatest commandment. Surely we need this type of reformation, to more fully love God and one another, to live the love we see in the example of Jesus.

Andrew Tucker

MAKING CONNECTIONS

- Consider how the story of Moses at the edge of the promised land might relate to Jan Hus, a reformer who never saw the fullness of the Reformation, as well as to Luther, whose desire for a Catholic reformation led instead to his excommunication by Rome.
- Use projection or print samples of Reformation-era art, like that of Lucas Cranach, to help highlight these passages and themes.
- Include in the prayers examples of neighbor love needed in your community and how love of God might inspire that work.
- Lift up the unassuming members of your community who, like Paul to the Thessalonian community, selflessly reveal the interdependence of loving God and loving neighbors.
- Invite children to reflect on their actions for love of God (prayer, offering) and love of neighbor (sharing toys, speaking kindly). Invite them to practice those habits in the opposite direction—loving and helping our neighbors reflects our love of God—to create art that reflects these behaviors, or put on a skit that helps to make this connection.

Reformation Sunday 2017

SAMPLE PRAYERS OF INTERCESSION

The prayers are prepared locally for each occasion. The following examples may be adapted or used as appropriate.

Open to the gifts of the Holy Spirit, we pray for the church, the world, and all of God's creation.
A brief silence.
We pray for the unity of your church. Free us to be Christ's one body, graciously receiving his life and boldly offering it to a world in need. Lord, in your mercy,
hear our prayer.
We pray for the renewal of creation: for a shared, plentiful harvest, for lands unable to bear fruit, for what is neglected or destroyed by our hand, and for the earth's advocates. Lord, in your mercy,
hear our prayer.
We pray for all nations of the world: for leaders of villages, cities, states, and nations, for lawmakers and judges, for teachers and students, and for all who work for peace. Lord, in your mercy,
hear our prayer.
We pray for those who seek refuge and strength: refugees, the imprisoned, and those bound by addictions or burdened by guilt. We pray for the ill or injured (*especially*). Lord, in your mercy,
hear our prayer.
We pray for continual reformation in this and every assembly. In new beginnings, impart wisdom. In established traditions, inspire creativity. In all ministries, revive our hope in the one who makes all things new. Lord, in your mercy,
hear our prayer.

Here other intercessions may be offered.
We give thanks for your saints. United with them in the covenant of baptism, increase our faith in your promised life for all. Lord, in your mercy,
hear our prayer.
Into your hands, gracious God, we commend all for whom we pray, trusting the power of Christ and the gifts of the Spirit.
Amen.

PREACHING IDEAS
From a Scholar

The indignant retort, we "have never been slaves to anyone," in John 8:33 offers a glimpse of selective memory. We may want to respond: "Hmmm, aren't we forgetting Egypt? What about the Assyrian deportations? The Babylonian exile?" However, on this day, when we observe the 500th anniversary of the Reformation, perhaps John offers us a chance to take a closer look at our own selective memories. *How can we be honest about our own freedoms and our own enslavements?* Could such honesty be a true testament to Luther's 1520 "On Christian Freedom," where he wrote that a "Christian man is the most free lord of all, and subject to none; a Christian man is the most dutiful servant of all, and subject to everyone"?

As we observe the 500th anniversary of the Reformation, how can we, as Lutherans, recognize our selective memory and broaden our recollection that Reformation events brought about both liberty *and* distress? Are we free enough to see ramifications of the ways the Reformation caused blessing and harm? For example, we could follow the lead of the 2010 Lutheran World Federation public repentance for sixteenth-century Lutheran persecutions of Anabaptists (https://www.lutheranworld.org/content/resource-healing-memories-reconciling-christ). This was a public and communal time to repent of our enslavement to sin, turn from historic oppression at our hands, receive forgiveness, and celebrate the new possibilities of healing relationships.

We continue to wrestle with the paradox that we are both slave and free as we ask ourselves, "Are we free enough to voluntarily expend/enslave ourselves on behalf of others?" Our courageous engagement with this paradox in our history and current lives grows out of our encounter with the triune God. We celebrate with John 8 that it is God who sets us free to act as God's people in the world. We worship our living God who is Three in One, who is hidden and revealed, and whose strength is known in weakness. In worship we are *gathered* to the life-giving font and table and *sent* by baptismal and eucharistic impulses. We witness how intertwined liturgy and life are when we remind ourselves of local saints, who engage the paradoxical freedom to serve and whose stories form tapestries of ongoing deliberation, inspiration, and faith.

Romans 3 assures us that we cannot view summiting the upward hill of works righteousness as salvific. Rather, we thrive in the justification received as a gift through Christ's blood. The cross, central to our every gathering, also orients us toward those to whom God is oriented—the lame, the thirsty, the blind, to name just a few from John's gospel.

God's saving covenant with us is dramatically portrayed in Jeremiah 31, where we encounter the unbreakable new covenant. It will not be written on fragile stone tablets. This new covenant will be written internally. The marks of this covenant will be a life formed in God. We will not recall this covenant via our mental memories; since this covenant has become body knowledge, we have no chance of forgetting—it is inscribed within the fabric of our being. We are God's, and God is our refuge from our enslavements and toward God's freedom.

Jan Rippentrop

From a Preacher

What shall we preach on this day? Is this a day to look backward or to lean forward? The 500th anniversary of the Reformation is surely something to celebrate. It is equally certain that Martin Luther would urge us to preach the gospel—and we hear good news in all three texts for this day. We are also reminded that our identity as Lutheran Christians isn't found in what we are *against* but in God's promise *for* us, setting us free to be *for* others.

God's word in Jeremiah 31 reminds us that the new covenant was made to "the people of Israel and Judah." We do not celebrate this day because Christians have replaced Jews as God's chosen people. We rejoice that God's covenant is also written on our hearts.

Romans 3:22-24 is, for many people, the memory passage of the Reformation: "For there is no distinction, since all have sinned and fall short of the glory of God; they are now justified by [God's] grace as a gift, through the redemption that is in Christ Jesus." But for centuries distinctions have torn the church apart. We do not celebrate because we are not Roman Catholic but because God's mercy is deeper than our divisions.

"You will know the truth, and the truth will make you free." Jesus' words in today's gospel are worth memorizing—as long as we remember that this truth isn't a bumper sticker affirming whatever we think is true. What happens when we hear these verses in their larger context? This chapter opens with religious leaders bringing a woman accused of adultery to Jesus. The accusers had the written law on their side. Jesus didn't argue. Instead, he bent down in silence and wrote on the ground. Then he said, "Let anyone among you who is without sin be the first to throw a stone at her." When he looked up, she alone was left. "Has no one condemned you?" Jesus asked. "No one, sir." "Neither do I condemn you," Jesus said. "Go your way, and from now on do not sin again." The truth bent down to be with a woman accused. The truth that sets us free is more powerful than the words written down. This truth set a woman free from death, free to turn her life around.

By the end of this chapter, the religious leaders have turned their stones against Jesus. Somehow he got away, but not for long. At Jesus' trial, Pilate asked him, "What is truth?" Jesus stood there in silence. This truth is not a proposition but a person.

"What is truth?" If the truth that sets us free is a person rather than a proposition, then Christ's body, the church, is a living, changing organism. We not only look back, we also lean forward. Where is God calling the church today? Church historian Rosemary Radford Ruether says there are two things the church must be organized to do: assure responsible transmission of the tradition from one generation to another, and be open to the winds of the Spirit by which the tradition can come alive (Rosemary Radford Ruether, *Women-Church: Theology and Practice of Feminist Liturgical Communities* [San Francisco: Harper & Row, 1985], 34). Both are essential. Throughout history the church has often tipped too far to one side. Sometimes new movements caught fire but failed to pass on anything to their children. They burned out and died. But sometimes tradition became so rigid that the Spirit couldn't find a crack to enter. When that happened, God called people to pound on the doors of the church or sit down in the front of the bus to reform institutions grown rigid.

We look back and we lean forward. When the Lutheran World Federation met in Windhoek, Namibia, in May, Lutherans from around the world focused on three themes:

- Salvation—Not for Sale: We look back to reclaim God's free gift of grace. But we also lean forward to discern where we are tempted to sell salvation with promises of wealth and success.
- Human Beings—Not for Sale: Every person is created in God's own image. We lean forward to stand against racism and whatever demeans God's beloved children.
- Creation—Not for Sale: In 1517 the reformers did not know that humans could destroy God's creation. We lean forward to protect the earth and all its creatures even though that calling seems impossible.
- We look back. We lean forward, never alone but trusting the one who bends down to be with us no matter how low we feel, no matter how challenging it is to be Christ's church in 2017.

Barbara Lundblad

MAKING CONNECTIONS

- Children: How much would you pay for God's love? (You might have some real or play money on hand.) $10? $100? $1 million? You don't need any money. God's love is free. So is God's forgiveness.
- How has the church changed since you were a child? What do you think needs to be reformed now?
- We're encouraged to earn a living, earn respect, win in sports and in business. How can we value God's *free* gift of grace?
- Flannery O'Connor has been quoted as saying, "You will know the truth, and the truth will make you odd." How is the church called to be odd in today's world?

THANKSGIVINGS
AT THE TABLE

ANNIVERSARY OF THE REFORMATION
A VARIABLE PRAYER FORM

This prayer is based on the readings appointed for Reformation Day: Jeremiah 31:31-34, Romans 3:19-28, and John 8:31-36. For an abbreviated prayer, use only the first line of each unit (A lines) placing a period where needed. For use on Sundays, use the first and the second line of each unit (A and B lines). For use on festivals, add an appropriate third line. Here the third lines, printed in italics (C lines), are especially appropriate for the 500th anniversary of the Reformation.

A   We praise you, all-holy God,
B   our maker, our lover, our keeper,
C   *our Covenant Lord, our Redeemer, the Strength of Truth,*

A   for the universe beyond our knowing,
B   for seas and forests and fields,
C   *for the waters of Wittenberg and for flowers in this place,*

A   for creatures seen and unseen,
B   for animals both wild and tame,
C   *for our ancestors and godparents from around the globe,*

A   and for the places we humans call home,
B   for cities and churches and schools,
C   *for seminaries and missions and fellowship halls.*

A   We praise you for your covenant people,
B   for Moses and Miriam and Aaron,
C   *for Jeremiah and the psalmists,*

A   and for centuries of faithful Christians,
B   for Mary Magdalene, Peter and Paul,
C   *for Luther, Melanchthon, Muhlenberg and Fedde,*
     for Katie Luther and Cranach, Bach and Nicolai,
     Nommensen and Kierkegaard,
     Bonhoeffer and Hammarskjöld,
     for all servants of the Reformation.

A   We praise you, O God, for Jesus Christ,

B   who saves us from sin and from evil,

C   *embodying forgiveness, granting us grace, setting us free,*

A   who on the night before he died,
took bread, and gave thanks; broke it,
and gave it to his disciples, saying:
Take and eat: this is my body, given for you.
Do this for the remembrance of me.

Again, after supper, he took the cup, gave thanks,
and gave it for all to drink, saying:
This cup is the new covenant in my blood,
shed for you and for all people for the forgiveness of sin.
Do this for the remembrance of me.

A   And so we remember your Word,

B   his life, his death, and his glorious resurrection,

C   *his presence in this meal around the world,*

A   and we proclaim the mystery of our faith:
Christ has died.
Christ is risen.
Christ will come again.

A   We pray, O God, for your Spirit,

B   your breath, your fire, your wisdom,

C   *your law, your grace, your freedom.*

A   Bless this meal and all those who share it;

B   inspire your people for service;

C   *continue the reformation of your churches;*

A   and renew the world with your mercy,

B   with your healing, your justice, and your peace,

C   *with the joy of life in your household.*

A   We praise you, all-holy God,

B   the Father, the Son, the Holy Spirit,

C   *mighty Fortress, victorious Champion, powerful Shield,*

A   today, tomorrow, and forever.
Amen!

A PRAYER FOR CHURCH ANNIVERSARIES

This prayer is based on the readings appointed for Reformation Day: Jeremiah 31:31-34, Romans 3:19-28, and John 8:31-36. Passages in italics are especially appropriate in giving thanks at the anniversary of the Reformation. These may be adapted for other church anniversary occasions.

O God before time, O God at the end,
we delight in the splendor of your universe.
Daily we laud your continuing creation,
and we give thanks *for all the homelands of your Reformation people.*
We glorify you, now and forever.
We glorify you, now and forever.

O God of the covenant, O God of the church,
we hear you speaking to centuries of your people.
We come as your children to this table,
and we give thanks for your presence *among Lutheran congregations around the world.*
We praise you, now and forever.
We praise you, now and forever.

You gave us Mary and Magdalene, Peter and Paul,
Luther and Melanchthon, Henry Muhlenberg and Elizabeth Fedde
— let us call out more names —
Katharina Luther the homemaker, Cranach the artist, Bach the musician,
Nicolai the hymnwriter, Nommensen the missionary, Kierkegaard the philosopher,
Bonhoeffer the martyr, Hammarskjöld the statesman,
countless other servants of the Reformation.
We bless you, now and forever.
We bless you, now and forever.

You came as Jesus, our wisdom, our guide,
embodying forgiveness, granting us grace, setting us free,
dying for sin, and alive for the life of the world.
We worship you, now and forever.
We worship you, now and forever.

In the night in which he was betrayed,
our Lord Jesus took bread, and gave thanks;
broke it, and gave it to his disciples, saying:
Take and eat; this is my body, given for you.
Do this for the remembrance of me.

Again, after supper, he took the cup, gave thanks,
and gave it for all to drink, saying:
This cup is the new covenant in my blood,
shed for you and for all people for the forgiveness of sin.
Do this for the remembrance of me.

Remembering his death, we cry out Amen.
Amen.
Celebrating his resurrection, we shout Amen.
Amen.
Trusting his presence in every time and place, we plead Amen.
Amen.

Come, Holy Spirit, and make here the body of Christ.
Breathe onto this food, that it bring us your life.
Empower your Reformation people throughout the world
to preach and teach, baptize and feed,
pray and sing, comfort and heal.
By your Spirit,
preserve what is faithful;
reform what we treasure;
create in us what is vital and new.
We honor you, now and forever.
We honor you, now and forever.

O God before time, O God at the end,
Father, Son, and Spirit,
we laud you,
Covenant Lord, our Redeemer, the Strength of truth.
Glory and praise, blessing and worship,
honor and power and might be to you, our God,
forever and ever.
Amen.

HYMNS FOR THE ANNIVERSARY YEAR

Probably every Lutheran congregation in the world will be singing "A mighty fortress is our God" on Reformation Sunday 2017. That chorale and hymns like "Lord, keep us steadfast in your Word" and "God's Word is our great heritage" are staples for any Reformation celebration, let alone the 500th. But what other hymns are particularly appropriate for use this year—not just in late October, but through-out the year? What follows are some suggestions from *Evangelical Lutheran Worship*, along with a few notes explaining why they were chosen. These hymns could be considered for scheduling in worship through the year, or some might be collected into a hymn festival.

It's worth noting what this list is not: it doesn't pretend to be a collection of the "best" hymns (whatever that might mean), or the ones with the strongest ties to the Lutheran Reformation. It was difficult to assemble this list because of all the worthy hymns, favorites of many, that had to be left out.

What is here is a sampling—some chorales, some hymns from other times and traditions, hymns from various places in the world. We hope you will consider them, but also that these will spur you to make your own selections from the treasury available. For more information about these hymns, please consult the marvelous *Hymnal Companion to Evangelical Lutheran Worship* by Paul Westermeyer, available from Augsburg Fortress.

Advent

ELW 243: LOST IN THE NIGHT
This hymn with roots in the Nordic countries of Finland, Norway, and Sweden captures well the longing of Advent, yet it also can be heard as expressing the church's deep and continuing need for enlightenment, to be released from sin and set free to help bring to "all peoples a Savior redeeming."

ELW 263: SAVIOR OF THE NATIONS, COME
For many, this ancient hymn is on the "must use every year" list already. It is included in this list because it embodies the Reformation: it was already a hymn of the church catholic, dating back to Ambrose in the fourth century. Then Martin Luther put it in the vernacular for Germans, at the same time subtly reshaping it, as all translations do. The hymn's strong gospel note carries through from Latin into English, reminding us that the good news of our salvation is a message shared by the whole Christian church.

Christmas

ELW 268: FROM HEAVEN ABOVE

Not much needs be said about this. It is Martin Luther's classic Christmas chorale, beautifully tells the story, and deserves to be known by every generation.

ELW 285: PEACE CAME TO EARTH

"The church must always be reformed" is one motto that will be heard a lot in this year. This hymn embodies that insight, being the product of two fairly recent Lutheran hymnic artists. The language, both text and music, shows the freshness of our times—note the perfect marriage of "gasp/sigh/see/pray" with an augmented fourth in the melody—but also conveys a clear evangelical message that would certainly win Martin Luther's approval.

ELW 287: LET ALL TOGETHER PRAISE OUR GOD

Paul Westermeyer's entry on this hymn in the *Hymnal Companion to Evangelical Lutheran Worship* explains why this hymn is well suited for use as we commemorate the Reformation: "The *fröhliche Wechsel*—the 'joyous exchange,' an expression Martin Luther used in connection with justification by grace through faith, is embedded in this hymn's fifth stanza. 'A wonderful exchange you make.'"

Time after Epiphany

ELW 309: THE ONLY SON FROM HEAVEN

With this hymn, another German chorale, we acknowledge the contributions of women to the early Reformation. Its author, Elizabeth Cruciger, was born into a noble family, then became a nun, left the monastery in the early 1520s, and married Caspar Cruciger, who became a professor at Wittenberg University. She was a friend of Katharina von Bora Luther.

ELW 313: O LORD, NOW LET YOUR SERVANT

In his beginnings of liturgical reform, Martin Luther sometimes suggested using hymn paraphrases for parts of the liturgy (see *Luther's Works*, vol. 53, pp. 49ff.) such as the Creed hymn (ELW 411) and the "Holy, holy, holy" hymn (ELW 868). "O Lord, now let your servant" continues this tradition, offering a paraphrase of Simeon's song ("Now, Lord, you let your servant go in peace") in a text by an American writer paired with a Finnish folk tune.

Lent

ELW 321: ETERNAL LORD OF LOVE, BEHOLD YOUR CHURCH

The Reformation is not just a Lutheran thing. In the decades and centuries after 1517, similar impulses took shape throughout western Europe. This strong hymn pays tribute to the whole church (even referring to our roots in the Jewish faith). Its author comes from the Anglican/Episcopal tradition, heirs of reformers like Thomas Cranmer, with a tune that originated in John Calvin's Geneva and the Reformed branch of the church.

ELW 340: A LAMB GOES UNCOMPLAINING FORTH

We are heirs to the gifts of thousands of hymn writers, both Lutheran and from other traditions. A few of these artists, though, have over time been recognized as preeminent—those whose hymns consistently show us God's grace in fresh, imaginative ways. Paul Gerhardt is on everyone's short list, and this beautiful hymn shows why. With an older tune by Wolfgang Dachstein, Gerhardt's text (here, four of the original ten stanzas) reveals the tenderness of God, the cross-bound love of Christ that permeates the Lenten season.

The Three Days

ELW 349: AH, HOLY JESUS

A favorite Lenten hymn, but does this have a Reformation connection? Yes, for two reasons. First, it is a collaboration between two of Lutheranism's foremost hymn producers, Johann Heermann (a pastor who, like Philipp Nicolai, endured great suffering while producing hymns like this) and composer Johann Crüger. Second, the text is so clear in enunciating the Reformation insights that we are, by ourselves, lost in sin, yet we are saved by the undeserved love of God in Christ.

Easter

ELW 364: CHRIST HAS ARISEN, ALLELUIA / *Mfurahini, haleluya*

The Lutheran church is, of course, a worldwide communion now, and the continent of Africa is its fastest-growing region. Among the countries with strong Lutheran presence are Zimbabwe, Madagascar, Nigeria, and Tanzania—the home of this lively celebration of Easter. The tune comes from the Haya people of northwestern Tanzania; the text, by retired pastor Bernard Kyamanywa, makes a strong statement of our resurrection faith.

ELW 370: CHRIST JESUS LAY IN DEATH'S STRONG BANDS

ELW 371: CHRISTIANS, TO THE PASCHAL VICTIM

ELW 372: CHRIST IS ARISEN

These three hymns are closely related and help sketch Reformation song from its Roman (Latin) roots (ELW 371), being transmuted as the Roman Catholic Church moved into Germany (ELW 372), and then showing Luther's work taking what was already there and adapting it for his purposes of helping the people worship and learn at the same time (ELW 370). See the *Hymnal Companion to Evangelical Lutheran Worship* for a fuller sketch of this transformation.

ELW 388: BE NOT AFRAID

Martin Luther, along with colleagues like Johann Walter and Joseph Klug, were intent that the music of worship be moved increasingly from specially trained choirs into the mouths of the worshiping assembly. That emphasis has continued over the centuries, and the gifts of Jacques Berthier and the ecumenical community of Taizé in France has helped in recent decades. Songs like this are simple to learn, best sung without instruments (as were the hymns in Luther's Wittenberg), and put the gospel into our mouths.

Pentecost

ELW 407: O LIVING BREATH OF GOD / *Soplo de Dios viviente*

In another demonstration of the multicultural church of which we are a part, here we have a text by a Roman Catholic Argentinean priest, translated by a Lutheran musician-professor. And the tune, which many assume is also Hispanic because of the text (and the nature of the tune), actually comes from Scandinavia—the Norwegians attribute it to Sweden, but it probably spans those borders. O living Breath of God, indeed!

Baptism

ELW 459: WADE IN THE WATER

Like all African American spirituals, this one has many layers. At its heart, though, this is a song about baptism. Martin Luther advocated that all Christians return daily to their baptism (see *Small Catechism*, "The Sacrament of Holy Baptism, IV, *ELW*, p. 1165). Though we are baptized once, again and again God "troubles the water." With its call-and-response structure, this song is eminently singable by the entire assembly.

Communion

ELW 479: WE COME TO THE HUNGRY FEAST

Martin Luther wrote voluminously in his lifetime. And the last words he wrote, a mere two sentences scribbled on some paper, could be said to sum up his theological insights: "We are beggars. This is true." This short hymn by Ray Makeever takes us in the same direction. We come to the communion feast hungry—begging for the love of God that will not be denied.

Word of God

ELW 519: OPEN YOUR EARS, O FAITHFUL PEOPLE

Martin Luther had his flaws, as he would be the first to acknowledge. Some that he didn't acknowledge were deeply hurtful to people even centuries later—witness the Nazis who used his diatribes against Jewish people as partial justification for the Holocaust. In view of this, it is fitting and poignant that Lutherans sing this beautiful hymn derived from Jewish sources as a call to listen to God's word of teaching, judgment, and life.

Time after Pentecost

ELW 414: HOLY GOD, WE PRAISE YOUR NAME

Many Lutherans probably think this hymn is one of ours—and it is, but in the sense that the church is not Lutheran or Methodist or Catholic, but finally catholic—that is, universal. One. And so we joyfully sing this paraphrase of the ancient Te Deum, even if it seems to have originated in Roman Catholic circles.

ELW 587, 588: THERE'S A WIDENESS IN GOD'S MERCY

Grace. If the Reformation had to be reduced to one word, it would probably be grace—the radical, completely undeserved love of God in Christ. Many hymns deal with the concept, but few as eloquently as this classic by Anglican priest Frederick Faber. The setting by twentieth-century composer Calvin Hampton is particularly beloved for the way it lyrically expresses the text.

ELW 600: OUT OF THE DEPTHS I CRY TO YOU

Luther used this hymn as an example of what he was looking for in biblically founded, grace-filled hymns. And this paraphrase of Psalm 130 is among the most poignant yet powerful hymns he wrote. Suitable for small group or even private devotion, this chorale has also inspired composers ever since, including several works by Johann Sebastian Bach.

ELW 641: ALL ARE WELCOME

The Reformation continues, still sounding its insistence that through God's grace, none are beyond the reach of forgiveness and acceptance; all are welcome. Here Lutheran-formed composer Marty Haugen, whose works are now widely sung and loved throughout the English-speaking church, expresses this foundational teaching in his winsome words and melody.

ELW 723: CANTICLE OF THE TURNING

Luther maintained a deep devotion to the Virgin Mary throughout his life, acknowledging her with the ancient title of *theotokos*, or bearer of God. Both Mary and Luther sang eloquently of God's work in putting down the mighty and lifting up the lowly, so this spirited paraphrase by American Rory Cooney, set to an Irish tune, can serve to commemorate them both and inspire us to follow in their path.

ELW 839, 840: NOW THANK WE ALL OUR GOD

Finally, there is only thanks. All we can offer to God is our thanks, our praise. We give thanks for Martin Luther and the other reformers. We give thanks for the Roman Catholic Church that nurtured him and still serves as a source of gospel light for millions. We give thanks for the whole church of all times and places, in all its varied expressions. With Martin Rinkhart and Johann Crüger and all the hymn writers, we give thanks to God—Father, Son, and Holy Spirit.

Robert Buckley Farlee

HYMN OF THE DAY AS REFORMATION INHERITANCE

In a Lutheran seminary course on Christian worship, a prominent professor had spent the full semester tracing the historical and theological roots of worship on the pattern of the Sunday assembly. He was particularly convincing with one of his many themes of the course: all Christian worship is derived from a common shape, which is an ecumenical inheritance. On the final day of class, when students were invited to ask any question, a Lutheran student asked, "What, then, makes Christian worship specifically Lutheran?" The professor paused a moment to collect an answer. Then he offered this: "I suppose it is the way Lutherans sing in Christian worship. But by 'the way we sing,' I do not mean necessarily the fervor of our singing or the grand repertoire of song available to us, or even the amount of music we sing in each service. I mean the purpose of our song is perhaps different. For instance, the placement and purpose of the hymn of the day are unique to Lutherans in the ecumenical shape of the Sunday and festival liturgy of holy communion."

The placement and purpose of a hymn that unites the proclamation of the scripture texts and preaching for the day with the spirit of the season and the contextual character of each assembly is a Reformation inheritance. This central hymn is a communal proclamation of the gospel, parallel to the proclamation of an address given to those who have been called to speak such a word on our behalf in sermons or homilies. According to the rubrics of *Evangelical Lutheran Worship*, the hymn of the day is a central element of the liturgy of holy communion (p. 92).

Before the Reformation, extrabiblical texts were sometimes added to the alleluia that was sung between the reading from the appointed epistle and gospel readings. These texts, called tropes or sequences, formed a repertoire of sung proclamation to be sung by the schola or choir. In Luther's modest reforms of the Mass, a hymn to be sung by the assembly invoking the Holy Spirit was placed between the assigned epistle and gospel readings. Further, a primary hymn chosen to correspond to the assigned scripture texts was placed either after the gospel reading and prior to the preaching or after the preaching of the sermon. By the time of J. S. Bach two hundred years later, this calendar of hymns appointed for every Sunday and festival of the one-year lectionary was established, such that the flourishing of works based on these appointed hymns resulted in cantatas and organ preludes.

As we commemorate the anniversary of the Reformation, it seems wise to recover this inheritance as fully as possible. Such a recovery would not mean that every congregation should use the same calendar of hymns at all times. Rather, each assembly could select the primary hymn of the day, chosen with the guidance of worship planning aids like *Sundays and Seasons*, and commit to singing at least this hymn each week. This primary hymn might also receive the most attention from the musicians and musical groups of the congregation.

In some places, this primary hymn of the day is called a sermon hymn. Such a title is limited, as it implies that the hymn relates only to the sermon and not the whole day's worship. It is easy to imagine, if the worship planning in a congregation is done largely by a pastor who will be asked to spend considerable time preparing a sermon for the liturgy, that he or she might want the hymn to correspond to the sermon as best as possible. However, a preacher cannot fully discern the movement of the Spirit in time to adequately name the primary hymn of the day for a liturgy, particularly if it is to receive the best support, leadership, and rendering of the musicians and the full assembly. It would be better to plan the list of the primary hymn of the day for each Sunday and festival of the year well in advance, even three, six, or ninth months in advance, to allow for thorough preparation. Then, when such a list is determined by the worship planners, a preacher can open the hymnal to the primary hymn and consult it as "richer fare" to open up the scriptures as the sermon is being prepared.

Mark Mummert

COMMON PRAYER
From Conflict to Communion:
Lutheran–Catholic
Common Commemoration
of the Reformation in 2017

Text by the Liturgical Task Force of the Lutheran–Roman Catholic Commission on Unity

Introduction to the Common Prayer for the Ecumenical Commemoration

COMMON PRAYER

This liturgical order marks a very special moment in the journey from conflict to communion between Lutherans and Catholics. It offers an opportunity to look back in thanksgiving and confession and look ahead, committing ourselves to common witness and continuing our journey together.

The ecumenical commemoration of five hundred years of reformation reflects in its basic liturgical structure this theme of thanksgiving, repentance, and common witness and commitment, as developed in *From Conflict to Communion: Lutheran–Catholic Common Commemoration of the Reformation in 2017: Report of the Lutheran–Roman Catholic Commission on Unity*. These characteristics of common prayer mirror the reality of Christian life: shaped by God's Word, the people are sent out in common witness and service. In this particular and unique ecumenical commemoration, thanksgiving and lament, joy and repentance mark the singing and the praying as we commemorate the gifts of the Reformation and ask forgiveness for the division that we have perpetuated. Thanksgiving and lament, however, do not stand alone: they lead us to common witness and commitment to each other and for the world.

A PRACTICAL GUIDE
Roles in the Common Prayer

Throughout this ecumenical commemoration, two roles are designated: presiders and readers. The two presiders are to be Lutheran and Catholic. The two readers are to be Catholic and Lutheran. The readers and presiders should not be the same persons.

In the second half of the common prayer, other readers and leaders of intercessory prayer will be called upon. These readers should not be the same as the main readers and presiders. Ecumenical guests, if present, can be invited to participate in these various roles.

Instructions for the Common Prayer

MUSIC

The songs suggested here are only given as examples. They are conceived for a multicultural context. Every context and language, every time and place will find hymns, chants, and songs that fulfill the same role in the prayer as these suggested ones. Choosing appropriate music begins with understanding the particular function of a song in the liturgy.

OPENING

The opening song may be a song that gathers us together in thanksgiving and in the name of the triune God. It can be either a classic hymn that is known to both Catholics and Lutherans or a new song. For example, "Praise to the Lord, the Almighty" ("Lobe den Herren"; ELW 858, 859) or a more recent song from Brazil, "Cantai ao Senhor" (Spanish "Cantad al Señor"; in English "O sing to the Lord"; ELW 822).

The opening dialogue includes two options. Communal prayer begins in various ways. In some regions it is standard practice to begin in the name of the triune God. In others it is more usual to begin prayer with "O Lord, open my lips . . ." followed by the naming of the triune God in the doxology. The presiders then welcome those gathered, inviting them into the basic action of the liturgy.

A reader then quotes from the study document *From Conflict to Communion*, which explicitly states why we are gathered as Lutherans and Catholics together. This passage also includes a reading from scripture (1 Cor. 12:26). A presider concludes this section in prayer, invoking the Holy Spirit.

After this opening and prayer, the assembly joins in song and calls on the Holy Spirit to illumine hearts and prayer. Songs that fulfill this role are, for example, "O living Breath of God/Soplo de Dios viviente" (ELW 407) or "Gracious Spirit, heed our pleading" (ELW 401) or more meditative songs in the style of Taizé (for example, "Veni Sancte Spiritus," ELW 406) or songs such as "Come Holy Spirit, Descend on Us" (Iona Community).

THANKSGIVING

After the opening, we look back together in thanksgiving and repentance. These two sections begin with readings and reflections from both the Catholic and the Lutheran side. The Thanksgiving section concludes with a prayer of thanksgiving and a song of thanksgiving. The repentance moves into confession, the singing of Psalm 130, the promise of forgiveness in Christ, and the sharing of peace.

The section titled "Thanksgiving" expresses our mutual joy for the gifts received and rediscovered in various ways through the renewal and impulses of the Reformation. After the prayer of thanksgiving, the whole assembly joins in singing thanks for and praise of God's work. Songs of praise familiar to all are best used here. Some examples include "Thanks Be to You Forever" (Marty Haugen) or "To God Our Thanks We Give" ("Reamo leboga" from Botswana; ELW 682) or "Laudate Dominum" (Taizé).

REPENTANCE

After two readings that help contextualize the confession, the presiders lead the assembly in a three-part prayer. First, the assembly laments the way in which even good actions of reform often had unintended negative consequences. Second, the assembly acknowledges the guilt of the past. Third, the assembly confesses its own complacency that has perpetuated the divisions of the past and has built more walls today. The assembly joins the presiders by responding to each section with a sung Kyrie eleison.

Psalm 130 ("Out of the depths") is then chanted. The entire psalm is recommended for use rather than paraphrases. There are many chanted versions of Psalm 130 available, including the plainchant found in most hymnbooks or more developed versions with antiphons and responsive singing (for example, see works by composers Gelineau, Farlee, Haugen, Joncas, and collections such as *Psalter for Worship* and *Psalm Settings for the Church Year*).

The psalm is followed by the promise of forgiveness in Christ that is jointly or alternately spoken by the presiders, who then invite the assembly into the sharing of peace and reconciliation. During the Sharing of the Peace, "Ubi caritas et amor" (Taizé; ELW 642) may be sung. This chant focuses on the theme of unity: where love and charity abide, God dwells there. On a more practical side, a repetitive song such as "Ubi caritas et amor" can be sung for as long as it takes for the assembly to share the peace.

COMMON WITNESS AND COMMITMENT

Thanksgiving and repentance lead the assembly into common witness, commitment, and service.

Following the peace, the assembly listens to the gospel read by one of the readers. The Gospel of John 15 places Jesus Christ at the center. Without Christ, we can do nothing. In response to the gospel reading, the presiders preach a joint sermon (see notes for the sermon).

The assembly professes their common faith in the words of the Apostles' Creed.

A song now moves the assembly from hearing the word into very specific commitments that come from the five imperatives found in *From Conflict to Communion*. The character of this song could focus the assembly toward service in the world. For example, "O Lord, we praise you" (Luther; ELW 499) or "Lord, keep us steadfast in your word" (Luther; ELW 517) or "We all are one in mission" (a Finnish tune; ELW 576). [Note: If the creed is sung, another song may not be necessary at this point, or it may be sung after the presider introduces the Five Commitments, "Our ecumenical journey continues. . . ."]

The five imperatives or commitments are announced in the assembly. Young people could read the commitments. After each reading, someone (maybe young children or families, especially families that represent ecumenical—Catholic/Lutheran—marriages) lights one of the five large candles that are either on the altar or in a beautiful arrangement near the altar. The paschal candle may serve as the main light from which the five other candles are lighted, reflecting in this way the gospel reading: apart from Christ, we can do nothing. The paschal candle may also be set next to the baptismal font.

After the five commitments have been read, a song of light is sung. For example, "Christ, Be Our Light" (Bernadette Farrell; ELW 715) or "Come Light, Light of God" (Community of Grandchamp, Switzerland) or "Kindle a Flame" (Iona Community) or "Within our darkest night, you kindle a fire that never dies away" (Taizé).

The assembly prays. The intercessions are addressed to God, whose mercy endures forever. They may be adapted to time and place, adding or editing intercessions as needed that address the local situation and the current world situation.

The concluding prayer leads into the Lord's Prayer.

Common prayer concludes with a thanksgiving[1] and blessing spoken by both presiders.

The song after the blessing sends us out with joy into the world. If this common prayer began with a well-known hymn from the tradition, this sending song could be a song composed recently that looks toward God's future. For example, if at the beginning, the assembly sang "Praise to the Lord, the Almighty," they might end with "Cantai ao Senhor" ("Oh, sing to the Lord").

SERMON NOTES

The sermon should reflect on the link between Jesus Christ as the center and fundament of the church (John 15) and the commemoration of five hundred years of the Reformation as part of the journey *From Conflict to Communion*, moving the gathered assembly to an ongoing commitment to common witness and service and to prayer for unity.

The commemoration of the Reformation should be a celebration of Jesus Christ, since the reformers saw their main task in pointing to Christ as "the way, the truth, and the life" and calling people to trust in Christ. Christ should be celebrated. Martin Luther and the other reformers only sought to be "witnesses to Christ."

Since the sermon (or the two sermons) should not be too long, the preacher(s) should focus on John 15 and its connection with the journey *From Conflict to Communion*, as described above. Elements of thanksgiving and repentance that were addressed earlier in the service may be taken as illustrations, as well as experiences from the respective congregations. However, there should not be too many topics. The sermon should have a clear line: it should lead to focusing on Christ, the witness to Christ, seeking the unity of the one vine, and being sent out in common service with and for others in communion with Christ.

Chapter 5 of *From Conflict to Communion* can be particularly helpful in establishing a structure for a joint sermon, for it provides several summary statements.

The preachers may also reflect on the Five Imperatives found in chapter 6. These imperatives could be developed with specific reference to the local context.

---

1   The concluding dialogue is reproduced by permission from *A Wee Worship Book 4* (Wild Goose Publications, 1999). Text (adapted) John L. Bell, © 1999 WGRG, c/o Iona Community, Glasgow G2 3DH, Scotland. www.wildgoose.scot.

The scriptural text is John 15:1-5.

- Christ calls himself "the true vine," but a vine cannot be without branches. Christ does not want to be without the church, as the church is nothing without Christ, and without Christ we can do nothing.

- There is only *one* true vine. All the branches are branches of *one* vine, and thus they are called to unity. As we come closer to Christ, we also come closer to each other. John's gospel focuses on communion with Christ, who is the face of the Father's mercy.

- The branches exist not for themselves but in order to bear fruit. The fruit is twofold: witness and service. Believers in Christ and the church as a whole are witnesses to the gift given to them. They are witnesses for the life with Christ and the salvation through Christ. The world that constantly forgets God desperately needs this witness. In communion with Christ we are called to serve others just as Christ serves us. In the present context, one important fruit of the branches is their longing for unity, seeking unity, being committed to continue the journey to unity. The imagery of the vine and branches is one of growth. On the ecumenical journey, we commit ourselves to growth, with all that growth entails.

- The branches are in constant need of being cleansed: *ecclesia semper reformanda*. The emphasis laid in John 15 on the fruits and the cleansing (or pruning) of the branches creates the challenge to us of self-critically examining ourselves. This also allows for coming back to the element of repentance in the service, but it should be more oriented to the future. We are called to be converted to Christ; we also are called to love and serve our neighbor. Following these callings will require that, through the power of the Holy Spirit, our own self-centeredness (and that of the churches) be overcome. Here the imperatives can be of some help in describing this call to conversion and to unity.

- At the heart of this text is the statement that without Christ we can do nothing. Christ is the center. Our journey of faith, our journey together, and our commitment to common witness and service all have their source in Jesus Christ.

- This communion or relationship is not only individual but communal. It is reflected in a common commitment and witness, in a common purpose and service in and for and with the world.

- "Oneness" in purpose and service witnesses to God, who is love. "That they may all be one so that the world may believe" (John 17:21).

- Abiding: Remaining in Christ implies remaining in fellowship with one another. It is in abiding or remaining in fellowship, committed to communion and reconciliation, that good fruit is produced. A good tree is recognized by its good fruit. A good tree is one that is not divided in itself.

Theo Dieter
Dirk Lange
Wolfgang Thönissen

Common Prayer

FROM CONFLICT TO COMMUNION: LUTHERAN—CATHOLIC COMMEMORATION OF THE REFORMATION

Opening

OPENING SONG

Presider I:
In the name of the Father, and of the ✝ Son, and of the Holy Spirit.
Amen.

The Lord be with you.
And also with you.

One of the following dialogues is spoken. Other opening dialogues may be used, depending on context and language.

O Lord, open my lips.
And my mouth shall proclaim your praise.

or
Glory to the Father, and to the Son, and to the Holy Spirit;
As it was in the beginning, is now, and will be forever. Amen.

Presider I:
Dear sisters and brothers in Christ! Welcome to this ecumenical prayer, which commemorates the five hundred years of the Reformation. For over fifty years, Lutherans and Catholics have been on a journey from conflict to communion. With joy we have come to recognize that what unites us is far greater than what divides us. On this journey, mutual understanding and trust have grown.

Presider II:
So it is possible for us to gather today. We come with different thoughts and feelings of thanksgiving and lament, joy and repentance, joy in the gospel and sorrow for division. We gather to commemorate in remembrance, in thanksgiving and confession, and in common witness and commitment.

Reader I:
In the document *From Conflict to Communion*, we read, "The church is the body of Christ. As there is only one Christ, so also he has only one body. Through baptism, human beings are made members of this body" [#219]. "Since Catholics and Lutherans are bound to one another in the body of Christ as members of it, then it is true of them what Paul says in First Corinthians 12:26: 'If one member suffers, all suffer together; if one member is honored, all rejoice together.' What affects one member of the body also affects all the others. For this reason, when Lutheran Christians remember the events that led to the particular formation of their churches, they do not wish to do so without their Catholic fellow Christians. In remembering with each other the beginning of the Reformation, they are taking their baptism seriously" [#221].

Presider I:
Let us pray.

Brief silence

Jesus Christ, Lord of the church, send your Holy Spirit! Illumine our hearts and heal our memories. O Holy Spirit: help us to rejoice in the gifts that have come to the church through the Reformation, prepare us to repent for the dividing walls that we, and our forebears, have built, and equip us for common witness and service in the world.
Amen.

SONG INVOKING THE HOLY SPIRIT

Thanksgiving

Reader I:
A reading from *From Conflict to Communion:*
"Lutherans are thankful in their hearts for what Luther and the other reformers made accessible to them: the understanding of the gospel of Jesus Christ and faith in him; the insight into the mystery of the triune God who gives himself to us human beings out of grace and who can be received only in full trust in the divine promise; the freedom and certainty that the gospel creates; in the love that comes from and is awakened by faith, and in the hope in life and death that faith brings with it; and in the living contact with the Holy Scripture, the catechisms, and hymns that draw faith into life" [#225], in the priesthood of all baptized believers and their calling for the common mission of the Church. "Lutherans . . . realize that what they are thanking God for is not a gift that they can claim only for themselves. They want to share this gift with all other Christians" [#226].

Reader II:
"Catholics and Lutherans have so much of the faith in common that they can . . . be thankful together" [#226]. Encouraged by the Second Vatican Council, Catholics "gladly acknowledge and esteem the truly Christian endowments from our common heritage, which are to be found among our separated brethren. It is right and salutary to recognize the riches of Christ and virtuous works in the lives of others who are bearing witness to Christ, sometimes even to the shedding of their blood. For God is always wonderful in his works and worthy of all praise" [*Unitatis Redintegratio*, chap. 1]. In this spirit, Catholics and Lutherans embrace each other as sisters and brothers in the Lord. Together they rejoice in the truly Christian gifts that they both have received and rediscovered in various ways through the renewal and impulses of the Reformation. These gifts are reason for thanksgiving.

"The ecumenical journey enables Lutherans and Catholics to appreciate together Martin Luther's insight into and spiritual experience of the gospel of the righteousness of God, which is also God's mercy" [#244].

Presider I:
Let us pray.

Brief silence

Thanks be to you, O God, for the many guiding theological and spiritual insights that we have all received through the Reformation. Thanks be to you for the good transformations and reforms that were set in motion by the Reformation or by struggling with its challenges. Thanks be to you for the proclamation of the gospel that occurred during the Reformation and that since then has strengthened countless people to live lives of faith in Jesus Christ.

Amen.

SONG OF THANKSGIVING

Repentance

Reader I:

A reading from *From Conflict to Communion*:

"As the commemoration in 2017 brings joy and gratitude to expression, so must it also allow room for both Lutherans and Catholics to experience the pain over failures and trespasses, guilt and sin in the persons and events that are being remembered" [#228]. "In the sixteenth century, Catholics and Lutherans frequently not only misunderstood but also exaggerated and caricatured their opponents in order to make them look ridiculous. They repeatedly violated the eighth commandment, which prohibits bearing false witness against one's neighbor" [#233].

Reader II:

Lutherans and Catholics often focused on what separated them from each other rather than looking for what united them. They accepted that the gospel was mixed with the political and economic interests of those in power. Their failures resulted in the deaths of hundreds of thousands of people. Families were torn apart, people imprisoned and tortured, wars fought, and religion and faith misused. Human beings suffered and the credibility of the gospel was undermined with consequences that still impact us today. We deeply regret the evil things that Catholics and Lutherans have mutually done to each other.

Presider I:

Let us pray.

Brief silence

Presider II:

O God of mercy, we lament that even good actions of reform and renewal had often unintended negative consequences.

Kyrie eleison. (Lord, have mercy.)

Presider I:

We bring before you the burdens of the guilt of the past when our forebears did not follow your will that all be one in the truth of the gospel.

Christe eleison. (Christ, have mercy.)

Presider II:

We confess our own ways of thinking and acting that perpetuate the divisions of the past. As communities and as individuals, we build many walls around us: mental, spiritual, physical, political walls that result in discrimination and violence. Forgive us, Lord.

Kyrie eleison. (Lord, have mercy.)

PSALM 130

The psalm can be sung on psalm tone or read by alternate whole verse.

Presiders I and II:

These words may be said alternately by presiders I and II.

Christ is the way, the truth and the life. He is our peace, who breaks down the walls that divide, who gives us, through the Holy Spirit, ever-new beginnings.

In Christ, we receive forgiveness and reconciliation and we are strengthened for a faithful and common witness in our time.

Amen.

THE PEACE

Presider II:

Let the peace of Christ rule in your hearts, since as members of one body you are called to peace. The peace of Christ be with you always.

And also with you.

Presider I:

Let us offer each other a sign of reconciliation and peace.

SHARING OF PEACE

During the sharing of peace, "Ubi caritas et amor" or another hymn may be sung.

Gospel

Reader I:

As we continue our journey from conflict to communion, let us hear the Gospel according to John.

"I am the true vine, and my Father is the vinegrower. He removes every branch in me that bears no fruit. Every branch that bears fruit he prunes to make it bear more fruit. You have already been cleansed by the word that I have spoken to you. Abide in me as I abide in you. Just as the branch cannot bear fruit by itself unless it abides in the vine, neither can you unless you abide in me. I am the vine, you are the branches. Those who abide in me and I in them bear much fruit, because apart from me you can do nothing." (John 15:1-5)

The gospel of the Lord.

Thanks be to God.

JOINT SERMON

Presider I:

Together, let us confess our faith.

THE APOSTLES' CREED

SONG

COMMITMENTS: FIVE IMPERATIVES

Presider II:

Our ecumenical journey continues. In this worship we commit ourselves to grow in communion. The five imperatives found in *From Conflict to Communion* will guide us.

A large candle is lighted after each commitment is read. The light may be taken each time from the paschal candle. Young people may be asked to read the five commitments, and the candles may be lit by children and families. The organ or other instrument may play the melody of a song such as "In the Lord I'll be ever thankful" (Taizé) or another song to accompany the lighting of the candles.

1. Our first commitment: Catholics and Lutherans should always begin from the perspective of unity and not from the point of view of division in order to strengthen what is held in common even though the differences are more easily seen and experienced. [#239]
Light a candle.

2. Our second commitment: Lutherans and Catholics must let themselves continuously be transformed by the encounter with the other and by the mutual witness of faith. [#240]
Light a candle.

3. Our third commitment: Catholics and Lutherans should again commit themselves to seek visible unity, to elaborate together what this means in concrete steps, and to strive repeatedly toward this goal. [#241]
Light a candle.

4. Our fourth commitment: Lutherans and Catholics should jointly rediscover the power of the gospel of Jesus Christ for our time. [#242]
Light a candle.

5. Our fifth commitment: Catholics and Lutherans should witness together to the mercy of God in proclamation and service to the world. [#243]
Light a candle.

SONG

INTERCESSORY PRAYER

The person praying the intercessions should be different from the previous readers.

"Ecumenical engagement for the unity of the church does not serve only the church but also the world so that the world may believe" [#243]. Let us now pray for the world, the church, and all those in need.

God of mercy, throughout history your goodness prevails. Open the hearts of all people to find you and your mercy that endures forever.
Hear our prayer.

God of peace, bend that which is inflexible, the barriers that divide, the attachments that thwart reconciliation. Bring peace in this world, especially in [*name countries, places*]. Restore wholeness among us and show us your mercy.
Hear our prayer.

God of justice, healer and redeemer, heal those who suffer from illness, poverty, and exclusion. Hasten justice for those suffering under the power of evil. Give new life to all and show us your mercy.
Hear our prayer.

God, rock and fortress, protect refugees, those without homes or security, all abandoned children. Help us always to defend human dignity. Show us your mercy.
Hear our prayer.

God, creator, all creation groans in expectation. Convert us from exploitation. Teach us to live in harmony with your creation. Show us your mercy.
Hear our prayer.

God of mercy, strengthen and protect those who are persecuted for faith in you and those of other faiths who suffer persecution. Give us the courage to profess our faith. Your mercy endures forever.
Hear our prayer.

God of life, heal painful memories; transform all complacency, indifference, and ignorance; pour out a spirit of reconciliation. Turn us to you and one another. Show us your mercy.
Hear our prayer.

God of love, your Son Jesus reveals the mystery of love among us. Strengthen the unity that you alone sustain in our diversity. Your mercy endures forever.
Hear our prayer.

God, our sustenance, bring us together at your eucharistic table; nurture within and among us a communion rooted in your love. Your mercy endures forever.
Hear our prayer.

Presider II:

In confidence that God hears our prayers for the needs of this world and for the unity of all Christians in their witness, let us pray as Jesus taught us.

THE LORD'S PRAYER

Our Father . . .

Presider I:

For all that God can do within us, for all that God can do without us,

Thanks be to God.

Presider II:

For all in whom Christ lived before us, for all in whom Christ lives beside us,

Thanks be to God.

Presider I:

For all the Spirit wants to bring us, for where the Spirit wants to send us,

Thanks be to God.

Presiders (jointly):

The blessing of God, Father, ✛ Son, and Holy Spirit, be with you on your way together, now and forever.

Amen.

SONG

Other songs may be sung or a postlude played as people leave.

ORACIÓN COMÚN
Del conflicto a la comunión: Conmemoración conjunta luterano–católico romana de la Reforma en el 2017

Texto elaborado por el comité de liturgia de la Comisión Luterano–Católico Romana sobre la Unidad

Introducción a la Oración Común para la Conmemoración Ecuménica

ORACIÓN COMÚN

Este orden litúrgico marca un momento muy especial en el camino del conflicto a la comunión entre luteran*os* y católic*os*. Nos ofrece la oportunidad de mirar al pasado con agradecimiento y arrepentimiento, y mirar hacia el futuro comprometiéndonos en un testimonio común y continuando nuestro caminar conjunto.

La conmemoración ecuménica de los 500 años de la Reforma refleja en su estructura litúrgica básica el tema de la acción de gracias, la confesión y el arrepentimiento, y el testimonio y compromiso común, tal como fuera desarrollado en *Del conflicto a la comunión: Conmemoración conjunta luterano–católico romana de la Reforma en el 2017. Informe de la Comisión Luterano–Católico Romana sobre la Unidad.* Estas características de la Oración Común reflejan la realidad de la vida cristiana: formadas por la palabra de Dios, las personas son enviadas a dar testimonio y servicio en común. En esta particular y señera conmemoración ecuménica, la acción de gracias y el lamento, el gozo y el arrepentimiento, sellan el canto y la oración con *los* que conmemoramos los dones de la Reforma, pidiendo perdón por la división que hemos perpetuado. La acción de gracias y el lamento, sin embargo, no son todo, pues nos conducen al testimonio común y al compromiso de *los* un*os* con *los* otr*os* y con el mundo.

UNA GUÍA PRÁCTICA
Roles en la Oración Común

Durante esta conmemoración ecuménica se señalan dos roles: oficiantes y quienes leen. Las dos personas oficiantes serán una luterana y la otra católico romana. Las dos personas que leen serán una católica y la otra luterana. Quienes leen y quienes ofician no deben ser las mismas personas.

En la segunda parte de la Oración Común se convocará a otras personas para leer y líderes para la oración de intercesión. Estas no deben ser *las* mismas que las y los lectores principales y las y los oficiantes. De contar con invitadas e invitados ecuménicos, podrá ofrecérseles participar de estos roles.

Instrucciones para la Oración Común

MÚSICA

Los cánticos e himnos que aquí se sugieren se ofrecen sólo como ejemplos. Están pensados especialmente para un contexto multicultural. Cada contexto y lengua, tiempo y lugar, encontrará los himnos, cánticos y canciones que cumplan la misma función en la Oración que los que aquí se proponen. La selección de la música apropiada comienza con la comprensión de la función particular de un cántico en la liturgia.

APERTURA

El himno de apertura puede ser un cántico que nos congrega en acción de gracias y en nombre del Dios Trino. Puede ser un himno clásico conocido tanto por congregaciones católicas como luteranas, o una canción nueva. Por ejemplo, "Alma, bendice al Señor" (Lobe den Herren) o una canción más reciente, como "Cantad al Señor" de Brasil.

El diálogo de apertura incluye dos opciones. La oración comunitaria comienza de diversas maneras, dependiendo del país y la cultura. En algunas regiones es práctica corriente comenzar en el nombre del Dios Trino. En otras, es más habitual empezar la oración con "Oh Señor, abre mis labios," seguida por la doxología en el nombre del Dios Trino. *Los* oficiantes entonces dan la bienvenida a la comunidad, invitándol*os* a participar de la acción básica de la liturgia. Acto seguido una persona lee un pasaje del documento de estudio *Del conflicto a la comunión* que declara explícitamente por qué nos hemos reunido junt*os* como lutean*os* y católic*os*. Este pasaje también incluye una lectura de las Escrituras (1 Corintios 12:26). Una de las personas oficiantes concluye esta sección con una oración de invocación al Espíritu Santo.

Después de la apertura y la oración, la asamblea se une en canto y pide al Espíritu Santo que ilumine los corazones y la oración. Algunos himnos que desempeñan esta función son, por ejemplo, "Soplo de Dios," o "Gracious Spirit, Heed Our Pleading," o cantos más meditativos al estilo de Taizé (por ejemplo, "Ven Espíritu de Dios"), o cánticos como "Come Holy Spirit, Descend on Us" (Comunidad de Iona).

ACCIÓN DE GRACIAS

Después de la apertura, recordamos conjuntamente el pasado con acción de gracias y arrepentimiento. Estas dos secciones comienzan con lecturas y reflexiones desde el lado católico y el luterano. La sección de acción de gracias concluye con una oración y un canto de acción de gracias. El arrepentimiento lleva a la confesión, el canto del Salmo 130, la promesa del perdón en Cristo y el saludo de la paz.

La sección titulada *Acción de gracias* expresa nuestro regocijo por los dones recibidos y redescubiertos de diversas maneras a través de la renovación e iniciativas de la Reforma. Después de la oración de acción de gracias, toda la asamblea se une cantando en gratitud y alabanza por la obra de Dios. Lo mejor sería incluir cánticos que sean familiares a toda la asamblea. Algunos ejemplos incluyen, "Thanks Be to You Forever" (Marty Haugen), o "To God Our Thanks We Give" ("Reamo leboga" de Botswana), o "Laudate Dominum" (Taizé).

ARREPENTIMIENTO

Luego de dos lecturas que ayuden a contextualizar la confesión, las y los oficiantes guían a la asamblea en oración, que consta de tres momentos. En primer lugar, la asamblea lamenta que incluso las buenas acciones reformadoras han tenido a menudo consecuencias negativas no intencionales. En segundo lugar, la asamblea reconoce la culpa del pasado. En tercer lugar, la asamblea confiesa su propia complacencia, que ha perpetuado las divisiones del pasado y levantado hoy más murallas. La asamblea se une a las y los oficiantes respondiendo a cada sección con un Kyrie eleison cantado.

A continuación se canta el Salmo 130 ("Desde las profundidades"). Se recomienda utilizar el salmo completo más que versiones parafraseadas. Existen muchas versiones cantadas del Salmo 130, incluyendo el canto llano presente en la mayoría de los himnarios, o versiones más elaboradas con antífonas y canto responsorial (por ejemplo, ver las obras de compositores como Gelineau, Farlee, Haugen, Joncas). Al salmo le sigue la promesa del perdón en Cristo, que es impartida conjunta o alternadamente por *los* oficiantes, quienes entonces invitan a la asamblea a compartir el saludo de la paz y la reconciliación. Durante el saludo de la paz se puede entonar "Ubi Caritas" (Taizé). Este cántico se centra en el tema de la unidad: donde hay amor y caridad, allí está Dios. Desde un punto de vista práctico, un cántico reiterativo como Ubi Caritas puede entonarse por el tiempo que dure el saludo de la paz.

COMPROMISO Y TESTIMONIO COMÚN

La acción de gracias y el arrepentimiento conducen a la asamblea hacia el testimonio, el compromiso y el servicio común.

Después del saludo de la paz, la asamblea escucha el evangelio leído por una de las personas lectoras. El texto de Juan 15 sitúa a Jesucristo en el centro. Sin Cristo, nada podemos hacer. En respuesta a la lectura del evangelio, las personas oficiantes predican un sermón conjunto (ver notas para el sermón).

La asamblea entonces profesa su fe común con las palabras del Credo de los Apóstoles.

Un cántico marca la transición desde la escucha de la Palabra a los compromisos específicos provenientes de los cinco imperativos expresados en *Del conflicto a la comunión*. La temática de este cántico podría enfocar la atención de la asamblea sobre el tema del servicio en el mundo. Por ejemplo, "O Lord, We Praise You" (Lutero) o "Sosténnos firmes" (Lutero) o "We All Are One in Mission" (una tonada finlandesa). [Nota: en caso de cantarse el Credo no sería necesario cantar otro himno en este momento, o puede cantarse un himno después de que la persona oficiante introduzca los cinco compromisos, "Nuestro camino ecuménico continúa."]

Se anuncian en la asamblea los cinco imperativos o compromisos. Los compromisos pueden ser leídos por jóvenes. Después de cada lectura alguien (tal vez niños o familias, especialmente familias que representan matrimonios católico-luteranos) enciende una de las cinco velas grandes en el altar o en un sitio adecuadamente preparado cerca del altar. Puede utilizarse la llama de un cirio pascual para encender las cinco velas, reflejando de esta manera el texto del evangelio: aparte de Cristo, nada podemos hacer. El cirio pascual puede estar ubicado junto a la pila bautismal.

Después de leídos los cinco compromisos, se entona un himno que haga referencia a la luz. Por ejemplo, "Christ, Be Our Light" (Bernadette Farrell), o "Come Light, Light of God" (Comunidad de Grandchamp, Suiza), o "Kindle a Flame" (Comunidad de Iona), o "En nuestra oscuridad" (Taizé).

La asamblea se une en oración. Las intercesiones se dirigen a Dios, cuya misericordia perdura por siempre. Pueden ser adaptadas al tiempo y el lugar, agregando o editando intercesiones que hagan referencia a la situación local y la situación mundial actual.

La oración de cierre conduce al Padrenuestro.

La Oración Común concluye con una acción de gracias[1] y bendición por parte de ambas personas oficiantes.

El canto después de la bendición nos envía con júbilo al mundo. Si la Oración Común comenzó con un himno tradicional bien conocido, el himno de envío podría ser un canto más reciente que fije nuestra mirada en el futuro de Dios. Por ejemplo, si al principio la asamblea cantó "Alma, bendice al Señor" ahora se podría concluir con "Cantad al Señor."

NOTAS PARA EL SERMÓN

El sermón debería reflexionar sobre la relación entre Jesucristo como centro y fundamento de la iglesia (Juan 15) y la conmemoración de los 500 años de la Reforma como parte del camino *Del conflicto a la comunión*, alentando a la asamblea hacia un compromiso continuo de servicio y testimonio común y a orar por la unidad.

La conmemoración de la Reforma debería ser una celebración de Jesucristo, puesto que los reformadores consideraron su tarea principal apuntar a Cristo como "el camino, la verdad y la vida" y llamar a las personas a confiar en Él. Es Cristo quien debería ser celebrado. Martín Lutero y los otros reformadores sólo aspiraban a ser «testigos de Cristo.»

Puesto que el sermón (o los dos sermones) no debería ser muy extenso(s), quien(es) predica(n) debería(n) centrarse en Juan 15 y su relación con el camino *Del conflicto a la comunión* como se describiera más arriba. Pueden tomarse como ilustración referencias hechas en la acción de gracias y el arrepentimiento durante el servicio, y asimismo mencionarse experiencias de las respectivas congregaciones. Sin embargo, el sermón no debería abarcar muchos temas. Debería tener un claro lineamiento: centrarnos en Cristo, el testimonio de Cristo, buscando la unidad de la única vid, y el envío en comunión con Cristo para el servicio común con y hacia otras personas.

El capítulo 5 de *Del conflicto a la comunión* puede ser especialmente útil en el delineamiento de una estructura para un sermón conjunto, ya que proporciona varias afirmaciones concisas.

Quienes predican pueden también reflexionar sobre los cinco imperativos que se encuentran en el capítulo 6. Estos imperativos podrían expandirse con referencias específicas al contexto local.

---

1   El diálogo final se reproduce con permiso de "A Wee Worship Book 4" (Wild Goose Publications 1999.) Texto (adaptado) John L. Bell, © 1999 WGRG, a/c Comunidad de Iona, Glasgow 3DH, Escocia. www.wildgoose.scot

El texto bíblico es Juan 15:1-5.

- Cristo hace referencia a sí mismo como "la vid verdadera," pero una vid no existe sin pámpanos: Cristo no quiere ser sin la iglesia, como la iglesia no es nada sin Cristo: sin Cristo, nada podemos hacer.
- Hay *una* sola vid verdadera. Todos los pámpanos son pámpanos de *una* vid, y por lo tanto llamados a la unidad. Al acercarnos a Cristo también nos acercamos a otras personas. El evangelio de Juan se centra en la comunión con Cristo, quien es el rostro de la misericordia del Padre.
- Los pámpanos no son fines en sí mismos sino que existen para dar frutos. El fruto es doble: testimonio y servicio. Quienes creen en Cristo y la iglesia en su conjunto son testigos del don que les ha sido otorgado. Son testigos de la vida con Cristo y la salvación por medio de Cristo. El mundo que continuamente se olvida de Dios necesita desesperadamente de este testimonio. En comunión con Cristo se nos llama a servir a las y los demás como Cristo lo hace con nosotros y nosotras. En el contexto actual un fruto importante de los pámpanos es su anhelo de unidad, búsqueda de la unidad, y compromiso a proseguir en el camino hacia la unidad. La imagen de la vid y los pámpanos es una imagen de crecimiento. En el camino ecuménico nos comprometemos al crecimiento, con todo lo que conlleva este proceso.
- Los pámpanos siempre necesitan ser limpiados: *ecclesia semper reformanda*. El énfasis sobre los frutos y la limpieza de los pámpanos en Juan 15 nos trae el reto del examen autocrítico. Esto también nos permite relacionarlo con el momento del arrepentimiento en el servicio, pero debería estar más orientado hacia el futuro: el llamado siempre renovado a la conversión a Cristo y al prójimo como la superación del egocentrismo propio de las personas (y también del egocentrismo de las iglesias) a través del poder del Espíritu Santo. Aquí los imperativos pueden ayudar en la descripción de este llamado a la conversión y a la unidad.
- En el corazón de este texto hallamos la afirmación de que sin Cristo nada podemos hacer. Cristo es el centro. Nuestro camino de fe, nuestro camino conjunto, nuestro compromiso con el testimonio y servicio en común, tienen su fuente en Jesucristo.
- Esta comunión o relación no es sólo individual sino comunitaria. Se refleja en un compromiso y testimonio común, en un propósito y servicio conjunto en, para y con el mundo.
- "Unidad" en propósito y servicio da testimonio del Dios que es amor. ". . . que también ellos sean uno en nosotros, para que el mundo crea . . ." (Juan 17:21).
- Permanecer: Permanecer en Cristo implica permanecer en mutua comunión. Nuestra persistencia en la comunión, comprometidos con la comunión y la reconciliación, es la que produce buenos frutos. Un buen árbol se reconoce por sus buenos frutos. Un buen árbol es aquel que no está dividido en sí mismo.

Theo Dieter
Dirk Lange
Wolfgang Thönissen

Oración Común

DEL CONFLICTO A LA COMMUNION: CONMEMORACIÓN CONJUNTA LUTERANO–CATÓLICO ROMANA DE LA REFORMA EN EL 2017

Apertura

HIMNO DE ENTRADA

Oficiante I:
En el nombre del Padre, y del ✝ Hijo, y del Espíritu Santo.
Amén.

El Señor sea con ustedes.
Y con tu espíritu.

Pueden utilizarse otros diálogos de apertura acorde al contexto.

Señor, abre mis labios
Y publicará mi boca tu alabanza.

Gloria al Padre, y al Hijo, y al Espíritu Santo;
Como era en el principio, ahora y siempre, por los siglos de los siglos.
Amén.

Oficiante I:
¡Queridas hermanas y hermanos en Cristo! Les damos la bienvenida a esta celebración ecuménica que conmemora los 500 años de la Reforma. Por más de 50 años luteranos y católicos han recorrido el camino del conflicto a la comunión. Con júbilo hemos llegado a reconocer que lo que nos une supera con mucho aquello que nos divide. En este caminar, han crecido la comprensión y la confianza mutuas.

Oficiante II:
Por ello, hoy es posible congregarnos. Nos acercamos con diferentes pensamientos y sentimientos de acción de gracias y lamento, júbilo y arrepentimiento, gozo en el evangelio y pena por la división. Nos congregamos para conmemorar en remembranza, en acción de gracias y confesión, y en testimonio y compromiso común.

Lector(a) I:
En el documento *Del conflicto a la comunión* leemos: "La iglesia es el cuerpo de Cristo. Y dado que solo hay un Cristo, así también él tiene solo un cuerpo. Mediante el bautismo, los seres humanos son constituidos en miembros de su cuerpo" [#219]. "Ya que tanto católicos como luteranos se encuentran unidos unos a otros en el Cuerpo de Cristo, del cual son miembros, se verifica en ellos lo que Pablo menciona en 1 Cor 12:26: "Si uno de los miembros sufre, los demás comparten su sufrimiento; y si uno de ellos recibe honor, los demás se alegran con él." Lo que afecta a un miembro del cuerpo afecta también a todos los demás. Por esta razón, cuando los cristianos luteranos recuerdan los acontecimientos que dieron lugar a la formación particular de sus iglesias, no desean hacerlo sin sus hermanas

y hermanos cristianos católicos. Al recordar unos con otros el principio de la Reforma, están tomando en serio su bautismo" [#221].

Oficiante I:
Oremos.

Breve silencio

¡Jesucristo, Señor de la iglesia, envíanos tu Espíritu Santo! Ilumina nuestros corazones y sana nuestros recuerdos. Oh Espíritu Santo, ayúdanos a reconocer con gozo los dones que la Reforma ha brindado a la Iglesia, prepáranos para arrepentirnos de las murallas divisorias que nosotros y nuestros antepasados hemos levantado, y apréstanos para el testimonio y servicio común en el mundo.
Amén.

HIMNO DE INVOCACIÓN AL ESPÍRITU SANTO

Acción de gracias

Lector(a) I:
Una lectura de *Del conflicto a la comunión*
"Los luteranos están agradecidos de corazón por lo que Lutero y otros reformadores les hicieron accesible: el entendimiento del evangelio de Jesucristo y la fe en él; el reconocimiento del misterio del Dios Trino, que se da a sí mismo para nosotros, los seres humanos, por gracia, y que solo puede ser recibido en la confianza total de la promesa divina; en el reconocimiento de la libertad y la certidumbre que el evangelio crea; en el amor que procede de y es despertado por la fe; en la esperanza frente a la vida y frente a la muerte que la fe trae consigo; y en el contacto vital con la Santa Escritura, los catecismos y los himnos que le dan vida a la fe" [#225], en el sacerdocio de todos los creyentes bautizados y en su llamado para la misión común de la iglesia. "Los luteranos . . . se dan cuenta de que aquello por lo que agradecen a Dios no es un don que pueden reclamar solo para sí mismos. Desean compartir este don con todos los otros cristianos" [#226].

Lector(a) II:
". . . los católicos y los luteranos tienen en su fe tanto en común que pueden . . . estar agradecidos ambos en conjunto . . ." [#226]. Alentados por el Concilio Vaticano II *los* católicos "con gozo, reconocen y aprecian los tesoros verdaderamente cristianos que, procedentes del patrimonio común, se encuentran en nuestros hermanos separados. Es justo y saludable reconocer las riquezas de Cristo y las virtudes en la vida de quienes dan testimonio de Cristo y, a veces, hasta el derramamiento de su sangre, porque Dios es siempre admirable y digno de admiración en sus obras" (*Unitatis Redintegratio*, Capítulo 1). En este espíritu, católicos y luteranos se abrazan como hermanas y hermanos en el Señor. Juntos se regocijan en los dones verdaderamente cristianos que ambos han recibido y redescubierto de maneras diversas a través de la renovación e iniciativas de la Reforma. Estos dones son motivo de agradecimiento.

"El caminar ecuménico hace posible que luteranos y católicos puedan apreciar juntos la visión de Martín Lutero y su experiencia espiritual acerca del evangelio de la justicia de Dios, que es a la vez su misericordia." [#244]

Oficiante I:
Oremos.

Breve silencio

Te damos gracias, oh Dios, por las muchas perspectivas teológicas y espirituales orientadoras que todos hemos recibido por medio de la Reforma. Te damos gracias por las transformaciones y cambios positivos desencadenados por la Reforma o por los desafíos que nos impuso. Te damos gracias por la proclamación del evangelio durante la época de la Reforma y que desde entonces ha fortalecido a innumerables personas a vivir vidas de fe en Jesucristo.
Amén.

HIMNO DE ACCIÓN DE GRACIAS

Arrepentimiento

Lector(a) I:
Una lectura de *Del conflicto a la comunión*
"Así como la conmemoración común en 2017 traerá expresiones de alegría y de gratitud, también deberá permitir un espacio para que tanto luteranos como católicos experimenten el dolor por los fracasos, las transgresiones, las culpas y los pecados relativos a las personas y acontecimientos que se conmemoran" [#228]. "En el siglo XVI, católicos y luteranos frecuentemente no solo malinterpretaron, sino que exageraron y caricaturizaron a sus oponentes para ridiculizarlos. Repetidamente violaron el octavo mandamiento, que prohíbe dar falso testimonio contra nuestro prójimo" [#233].

Lector(a) II:
Con frecuencia luteranos y católicos se han concentrado en lo que los separaba en lugar de lo que los unía. Aceptaron el hecho de que el evangelio estuviese atado a los intereses políticos y económicos de aquellos en el poder. Sus fracasos resultaron en la muerte de cientos de miles de personas. Hubo familias destruidas, personas encarceladas y torturadas, se libraron guerras y la religión y la fe fueron abusadas. Muchos seres humanos sufrieron y la credibilidad del evangelio fue socavada de tal manera que sus consecuencias todavía nos afectan. Lamentamos profundamente las iniquidades que católicos y luteranos se han infligido mutuamente.

Oficiante I:
Oremos.

Breve silencio

Oficiante II:
Oh Dios de misericordia, lamentamos que aún las buenas acciones de reforma y renovación hayan tenido a menudo consecuencias negativas no intencionales.
Kyrie eleison (Señor, ten piedad)

Oficiante I:

Traemos ante ti el peso de las culpas del pasado, cuando nuestros antepasados no siguieron tu voluntad de que todos sean uno en la verdad del evangelio.
Christe eleison (Cristo, ten piedad)

Oficiante II:

Confesamos nuestras propias formas de pensar y actuar que perpetúan las divisiones del pasado. Como comunidades y como individuos nos rodeamos de muchas murallas: mentales, espirituales, físicas y políticas, que resultan en discriminación y violencia. Señor, perdónanos.
Kyrie eleison (Señor, ten piedad)

SALMO 130

El salmo puede cantarse o leerse sus versículos en forma alternada.

Oficiantes I y II:

Estas líneas pueden ser leídas alternadamente por los oficiantes I y II.

Cristo es el camino, la verdad y la vida. Él es nuestra paz, quien derriba las murallas que nos dividen, quien nos concede, a través del Espíritu Santo, renovados comienzos.

En Cristo recibimos perdón y reconciliación, y se nos fortalece para un testimonio común y fiel en nuestros tiempos.
Amén.

LA PAZ

Oficiante II:

Que la paz de Cristo reine en sus corazones, pues como miembros de un solo cuerpo se les llama a la paz. La paz de Cristo sea siempre con ustedes.
Y con tu espíritu.

Oficiante I:

Compartamos unos con otros una señal de reconciliación y paz.

SALUDO DE LA PAZ

Durante el saludo puede cantarse Ubi Caritas u otro himno.

Evangelio

Lector(a) I:

Continuando nuestro camino del conflicto a la comunión, escuchemos el evangelio según San Juan.

Yo soy la vid verdadera y mi Padre es el labrador. Todo pámpano que en mí no lleva fruto, lo quitará; y todo aquel que lleva fruto, lo limpiará, para que lleve más fruto. Ya vosotros estáis limpios por la palabra que os he hablado. Permaneced en mí, y yo en vosotros. Como el pámpano no puede llevar fruto por sí mismo, si no permanece en la vid, así tampoco vosotros, si no permanecéis en mí. Yo soy la vid, vosotros los pámpanos; el que permanece en mí y yo en él, éste lleva mucho fruto, porque separados de mí nada podéis hacer. (Juan 15:1-5)

El Evangelio del Señor.
Demos gracias a Dios.

SERMÓN CONJUNTO

Oficiante I:
En conjunto, confesemos nuestra fe.

EL CREDO APOSTÓLICO

HIMNO

COMPROMISOS: CINCO IMPERATIVOS

Oficiante II:
Nuestro camino ecuménico continúa. En esta celebración nos comprometemos a crecer en comunión. Nos guiarán los cinco imperativos presentes en *Del conflicto a la comunión*.

Después de la lectura de cada compromiso se enciende una vela. Para encender cada vela puede utilizarse la llama de un cirio pascual. Se puede solicitar a jóvenes la lectura de los cinco compromisos, y las velas pueden ser encendidas por niños y familias. Acompañando el encendido de las velas puede interpretarse en el órgano o en otro instrumento la melodía de un himno como "El Señor es mi fortaleza" (Taizé) o similar.

1. Nuestro primer compromiso: Católicos y luteranos deben comenzar siempre desde la perspectiva de la unidad y no desde el punto de vista de la división, para de este modo fortalecer lo que mantienen en común, aunque las diferencias sean más fáciles de ver y experimentar. [#238]
Se enciende una vela

2. Nuestro segundo compromiso: Luteranos y católicos deben dejarse transformar a sí mismos continuamente mediante el encuentro de los unos con los otros y por el mutuo testimonio de fe. [#239]
Se enciende una vela

3. Nuestro tercer compromiso: Católicos y luteranos deben comprometerse otra vez en la búsqueda de la unidad visible, para elaborar juntos lo que esto significa en pasos concretos y esforzarse continuamente hacia esa meta. [#241]
Se enciende una vela

4. Nuestro cuarto compromiso: Luteranos y católicos deben juntamente redescubrir el poder del evangelio de Jesucristo para nuestro tiempo. [#242]
Se enciende una vela

5. Nuestro quinto compromiso: Católicos y luteranos deben dar testimonio común de la misericordia de Dios en la proclamación y el servicio al mundo. [#243]
Se enciende una vela

HIMNO

ORACIÓN DE INTERCESIÓN
La persona que lea las oraciones puede ser distinta de quienes leyeron previamente.

Oficiante I:
"El compromiso ecuménico para la unidad de la iglesia no solo sirve a la iglesia, sino también al mundo, para que el mundo crea" [#243]. Oremos ahora por el mundo, la iglesia, y por aquel*los* en necesidad.

Dios de misericordia, tu bondad prevalece a lo largo de la historia, abre los corazones de todas las personas para que te encuentren a ti y tu misericordia que perdura por siempre.
Escucha nuestra oración.

Dios de paz, doblega lo inflexible, las barreras que dividen, las adhesiones que frustran la reconciliación. Trae la paz a este mundo, especialmente a *[nombres de países o lugares]*. Restablece nuestra integridad y muéstranos tu misericordia.
Escucha nuestra oración.

Dios de justicia, sanidad y redención, sana a quienes sufren enfermedad, pobreza y exclusión. Que llegue la justicia para quienes sufren bajo el poder del mal. Otorga a tod*os* vida nueva y muéstranos tu misericordia.
Escucha nuestra oración.

Dios, roca y fortaleza, protege a las personas refugiadas, a quienes no tienen hogar o seguridad, a todos los niños y niñas abandonad*os*. Ayúdanos a defender siempre la dignidad humana. Muéstranos tu misericordia.
Escucha nuestra oración

Dios creador, toda la creación gime expectante, apártanos de la explotación. Enséñanos a vivir en armonía con tu creación. Muéstranos tu misericordia.
Escucha nuestra oración.

Dios de misericordia, fortalece y protege a quienes sufren persecución por su fe en ti y a las personas de otras creencias que son perseguidas. Otórganos el coraje para profesar nuestra fe. Tu misericordia perdura por siempre.
Escucha nuestra oración.

Dios de vida, sana los recuerdos dolorosos, transforma toda complacencia, indiferencia e ignorancia, derrama un espíritu de reconciliación. Vuélvenos hacia ti y hacia las y *los* otr*os*. Muéstranos tu misericordia.
Escucha nuestra oración.

Dios de amor, tu hijo Jesús revela el misterio del amor entre noso*tros*, fortalece esa unidad que solo tú sostienes en nuestra diversidad. Tu misericordia perdura por siempre.
Escucha nuestra oración.

Dios nuestro sustento, congréganos en tu mesa eucarística, nutre en y entre noso*tros* una comunión fundada en tu amor. Tu misericordia perdura por siempre.
Escucha nuestra oración.

Oficiante II:

En la confianza de que tú, oh Dios, escuchas nuestras oraciones por las necesidades de este mundo y por la unidad de todos los cristiano*s* y cristianas en su testimonio, oramos como Jesús nos enseñó. . . .

PADRENUESTRO

Padre nuestro . . .

Oficiante I:

Por todo lo que Dios puede hacer en noso*tros*, por todo lo que Dios puede hacer fuera de noso*tros*,
Demos gracias a Dios.

Oficiante II:

Por todas las personas en quienes Cristo vivió antes que noso*tros*, por todas las personas en quienes Cristo vive junto a noso*tros*,
Demos gracias a Dios.

Oficiante I:

Por todo lo que el Espíritu nos quiere ofrecer, por donde el Espíritu nos quiere enviar,
Demos gracias a Dios.

Oficiantes (juntos):

La bendición de Dios Padre, ✛ Hijo y Espíritu Santo sea con todos y todas ustedes y los y las acompañe en su camino conjunto, ahora y siempre.
Amén.

HIMNO

EVENING PRAYER

ORACIÓN DE LA TARDE

We may listen to drumming or other music.

We attend to the sound of a bell or gong.

We light a candle.

We sing an evening song.

We pray with words inspired by Psalm 121.

My help comes from you, O God,
you made heaven and earth.

You do not let my foot be moved,
you watch over me.

You are my keeper, my shade,
the sun shall not strike me by day,
nor the moon by night.

You preserve me from all evil,
you keep my life.

You watch over my going out
and my coming in,
from evening until morning,
now and always. Amen.

We listen to a short reading of scripture.

We meditate in silence.

God, our creator and protector,
you illumine the world and breathe life into us.
You heal the world with your outstretched arms.
You rescue creation and inspire your church.
We thank you for this day.

Podemos hacer oír el tambor u otra música.

Escuchamos el sonido de la campana o del gong.

Escendemos el cirio.

Cantamos un cántico vespertino.

Hacemos oración inspirada en el Salmo 121.

Mi socorro viene de ti, Oh Dios,
que has hecho el cielo y la tierra.

No dejas que mi pie se deslice,
tú velas sobre mí.

Tú eres mi guarda, mi sombra,
el sol no me herirá de día,
ni la luna de noche.

Tú me proteges de todo mal,
guardas mi vida.

Tú cuidas de mi salida
y de mi entrada,
desde el atardecer hasta el amanecer,
ahora y siempre. Amén.

Escuchamos una breve lectura bíblica.

Meditamos en silencio.

Dios, creador y protector,
tú iluminas el mundo e infundes vida en nosotros.
Sanas al mundo con tus brazos extendidos.
Rescatas la creación e inspiras a tu iglesia.
Te damos gracias por este día.

Let us remember your gifts and your promises
in our thoughts and actions,
in our communities and churches.
Amen.

On our hearts and on our houses,
the blessing of God.

In our coming and our going,
the peace of God.

In our life and our believing,
the love of God.

At our end and new beginning,
**the arms of God to welcome us
and bring us home. Amen.**

*After the final bell or gong the candle is
extinguished.*

Haznos recordar tus dones y tus promesas
en nuestros pensamientos y acciones,
en nuestras comunidades e iglesias.
Amén.

En nuestros corazones y casas,
haya bendición de Dios.

En nuestro ir y venir,
haya paz de Dios.

En nuestra vida y en nuestro creer,
haya amor de Dios.

En nuestro final y en nuestro nuevo comienzo,
**estén los brazos de Dios para recibirnos
y llevarnos al hogar. Amén.**

*Después de sonido final de la campana o del gong,
se extingue el cirio.*

A MIDWEEK LENTEN SERIES BASED ON LUTHER'S SMALL CATECHISM

INTRODUCTION

The year 2017 marks the international observance of the 500th anniversary of the Reformation. In honor of that anniversary, this midweek Lenten series is built around Luther's Small Catechism. The Small Catechism was designed as a teaching tool of the faith, not just within the church but in the home. Luther intended for the home to be the place where faith was first shared and taught. To that end he created the Small Catechism—a simple explanation of the Ten Commandments, the Creed, the Lord's Prayer, and the sacraments. He included basic prayers for morning and evening, and suggested ways to worship, praise, and revere God during each part of our day.

This series uses scripture readings from the daily lectionary (usually those appointed for the Wednesdays of each week in Lent) or passages referred to in the Small Catechism itself. The daily lectionary readings for year A are listed in *Evangelical Lutheran Worship*, pages 1121–25; the Small Catechism is printed on pages 1160–67. The first week of this series sets the stage with the handing down of the Ten Commandments in Exodus. The following weeks look at each major section of the Small Catechism in turn: the Creed, the Lord's Prayer, baptism, and holy communion. Studying the Small Catechism offers a way of growing closer to God by thinking on God's word and the basics of our faith. If desired, congregations could supplement this series with a weekly study of that portion of the catechism or use each portion in turn as part of the reflection.

FOR THE REFLECTIONS

Various forms of reflection may follow the scripture reading, such as brief commentary, teaching, or personal witness; nonbiblical readings; interpretation through music or other art forms; or guided conversation among those present. Commentary or teaching could connect scripture with the portion of the Small Catechism being featured each week. Or, the congregation could experience some kind of hands-on project together that follows the theme of the week. For example:

- Creating posters, either for the worship space or as family groups to take home, that match each week's portion of the Small Catechism. For example, the first week the poster could be as simple as copying the Ten Commandments (or Luther's explanations) or having each group paraphrase the commandments and put Luther's explanation into their own words. At the end of the five weeks, the community, or each group, would have posters on the entire Small Catechism.

- If you have longtime Lutherans in your congregation/community, ask them to bring in copies of the Small Catechism in different languages or earlier editions. Comparing them can spark intergenerational discussion.

- How would the different sections of the Small Catechism work as blog posts, on social media sites, or as brief video skits? Groups could create tweets, one-minute videos, raps, or whatever fits your local context.

OVERVIEW

Week of Lent 1—Ten Commandments

In Exodus God gives Moses the Law so that the people of Israel would know how to fulfill their part of God's covenant as God's people.

Link to Lent 1

The reading for this week comes from the daily lectionary, Wednesday of Lent 1, year A (*ELW*, p. 1123). If desired the reflection can also link to the psalm for the first Sunday in Lent, Psalm 32.

Week of Lent 2—Creed

How do we express belief? How do we share our faith? The Creed, crafted in the early days of the church, gives us a simple but firm foundation for sharing and professing.

Link to Lent 2

In Ezekiel, God promises Israel: "I will put my spirit within you, and make you follow my statutes and be careful to observe my ordinances" (36:27). The Creed reminds us of those ordinances, and how and why we are given the precious gifts of faith and belief by our loving God.

Week of Lent 3—Lord's Prayer

Lent and Lenten worship call us to repent, to make a new beginning. One of the best ways to begin again with God is through conversation, also known as prayer. And what better prayer than the one that Jesus taught us?

Link to Lent 3

In Psalm 81 God yearns for Israel to turn from their ways and follow God. When the disciples asked Jesus how to pray, he gave them, and us, the Lord's Prayer in Luke 11:1-4 (see also Matthew 6:9-13). In Luther's explanation of this prayer, he beautifully tells us not only what not to do but expands on how to live in the way God desires.

Week of Lent 4—Baptism

Dying to our old, sinful self in baptism, we rise from the waters as beloved children of God. We are walking wet throughout the forty days of Lent, reminded daily that we are dead to sin.

Link to Lent 4

In Psalm 23 the psalmist claims the promise to live in God's house forever. We too are given that promise in baptism, as Paul reminds us in Romans 6:3-5. Martin Luther uses this passage in the Small Catechism to tell us that we are "drowned" so that a new person may rise every day in God's service.

Week of Lent 5—Holy Communion

As we approach Holy Week, we remember Jesus' sacrifice for us. We gather around the table to remind ourselves and one another of that sacrifice and how it shapes our lives.

Link to Lent 5

In Psalm 143 the psalmist thirsts for God, asking to be revived. In holy communion we are revived and renewed with God's gifts of life and salvation. Luther reminds us that all we need is faith to make us worthy and well prepared to receive that gift.

OPENING DIALOGUE

Week 1

We begin in the name of the Lord, whom we are to fear and love.

Fear God? Are we to be afraid of our Creator?

Not afraid, but filled with reverent awe.

How shall we do this?

By trusting God above all things, and calling on God's name.

In every time of need, in prayer, praise, and thanks.

And because we fear and love God, we love and respect all God's creation.

People and animals, plants and water, mountains and deserts.

Week 2

We begin in the name of God,

Father, Son, and Holy Spirit.

What does this mean, this belief?

I believe that God has created me together with all that exists.

God daily and abundantly provides for me.

We confess that Jesus is Lord.

He has redeemed and freed us, so that we may belong to him.

How is this possible when we are who we are?

We believe because the Holy Spirit calls us.

Called, gathered, enlightened, and made holy, we praise God.

This is most certainly true!

Week 3

Behold, Lord, an empty vessel that needs to be filled.

My Lord, fill it.

I am weak in the faith;

strengthen me.

I am cold in love;

warm me and make me fervent,

that my love may go out to my neighbor.

I do not have a strong and firm faith;

at times I doubt and am unable to trust you altogether.

O Lord, help me.

Strengthen my faith and trust in you.

Week 4

We begin in the name of the Father,

and of the [✝] Son, and of the Holy Spirit.

The name in which we baptize.
What is baptism?
It is water used according to God's command
and connected with God's word.
What gifts does baptism grant?
It brings about forgiveness of sins, redeems from death,
and gives eternal salvation to all who believe.
How can water do such great things?
The water does not do this alone,
but the word of God with and alongside of the water, and faith.
This is a grace-filled water of life.
A bath of new birth in the Holy Spirit.

Week 5

Bless the Lord, who forgives all our sins.
God's mercy endures forever.
Blessed be God, who gives us life and salvation.
A gift we can never deserve or earn.
Given for you, for me, for all for the forgiveness of sins
in bread and wine, body and blood, words and presence.
Given in grace, received by faith.
Give us truly believing hearts, O God,
so that we might receive this great gift.

GATHERING SONG

ELW = *Evangelical Lutheran Worship*; WOV = *With One Voice*; LBW = *Lutheran Book of Worship*; TFF = *This Far by Faith*; W&P = *Worship and Praise*

Week 1

The glory of these forty days (ELW 320, WOV 657)
I'm going on a journey (ELW 446, TFF 115)

Week 2

Holy God, we praise your name (ELW 414, LBW 535)
Come, join the dance of Trinity (ELW 412)

Week 3

Our Father, God in heaven above (ELW 746/747)
Lord, listen to your children praying (ELW 752, TFF 247, WOV 775, W&P 92)

Week 4

As the deer runs to the river (ELW 331)
Jesus is a rock in a weary land (ELW 333)

Week 5

Jesus, still lead on (ELW 624, LBW 341)

My song is love unknown (ELW 343, WOV 661, LBW 94)

READING

Week 1: Exodus 34:1-9, 27-28

Week 2: Ezekiel 36:22-32

Week 3: Matthew 9:6-15

Week 4: Romans 6:1-14

Week 5: Matthew 26:26-29 *or* Luke 22:14-20

REFLECTION

The reading of scripture is followed by silence for reflection. Other forms of reflection may also follow, such as brief commentary, teaching, or personal witness; nonbiblical readings; interpretation through music or other art forms; or guided conversation among those present.

SONG

Week 1

If you but trust in God to guide you (ELW 769, LBW 453)

Week 2

I bind unto myself today (ELW 450, LBW 188)

Week 3

Oh, love, how deep (ELW 322, LBW 88)

Week 4

The King of love, my shepherd is (ELW 502, LBW 456)

Week 5

In the cross of Christ I glory (ELW 324, LBW 104)

LUTHER'S EVENING BLESSING

We give thanks to you, heavenly Father,

through Jesus Christ your dear Son, that you have graciously protected us today. We ask you to forgive us all our sins, where we have done wrong, and graciously to protect us tonight. Into your hands we commend myself: our bodies, our souls, and all that is ours. Let your holy angels be with us, so that the wicked foe may have no power over us. Amen.

LORD'S PRAYER

BLESSING
God the Father, ✝ Son, and Holy Spirit watch over us all.
Amen.

SENDING SONG
Week 1
Bless now, O God, the journey (ELW 326)

Week 2
Restore in us, O God (ELW 328, WOV 662)

Week 3
All praise to thee, my God, this night (ELW 565, LBW 278)

Week 4
Christ, the life of all the living (ELW 339, LBW 97)

Week 5
Jesus, keep me near the cross (ELW 335, TFF 73)

ACKNOWLEDGMENTS
The opening dialogues for weeks 2, 4, and 5 include adaptations or paraphrases of the text of the Small Catechism as presented in *Evangelical Lutheran Worship*, pages 1160–67. The opening dialogue for week 3 is a prayer of Martin Luther, *Evangelical Lutheran Worship*, page 87. Luther's Evening Blessing is from the Small Catechism, as adapted for Evening Prayer.

Lynn Bulock

THE CHURCH'S JOURNEY IN ART AND SONG
How to Adapt and Contextualize a Festival of Art and Music for Local Use during 2017 and beyond

It is often said that the Lutheran Church is a singing church. Singing by the gathered people of God, while not unique to Lutherans, is a hallmark of who we are. Lutherans have a rich tradition of the visual arts as well, dating back to Lucas Cranach. In a Lutheran understanding, both of these artistic forms can rightly be used to communicate the word of God and, therefore, when joined together, can be a rich way of commemorating the 500th anniversary of the Lutheran Reformation. However, music and visual art did not begin in sixteenth-century Germany, nor did they end there. These art forms are lively and ever evolving. We do well, therefore, to integrate music and art from many times, places, and peoples, moved by the same Spirit, to fully observe this forthcoming anniversary.

What is offered here is one possible plan that may be adapted for your unique context. It is meant to spark imagination and provide a starting point for creativity with integrity. A brief description of the core plan is presented here, along with some of the goals that guided its development. Extensive suggestions for adaptation and additional helps are included on the CD that accompanies this book.

Participants in the ELCA's 2015 Worship Jubilee, "Called to Be a Living Voice," gathered at Peachtree Road United Methodist Church in Atlanta to experience the first manifestation of this journey. An archive of the live-streaming from that event is being made available; information may be found at elca.org/worship. This may be helpful in understanding the flow of the core plan, hearing how some of the music might sound, and sparking the imagination.

A primary goal was to present the music and visual art in a thematic organization around the nature of the church and the Reformation, rather than in a historical or linear fashion. The three statements that guided the program development are:
1. The Spirit gathers the church around word and sacrament.
2. God hears our cries for mercy and pours out abundant grace.
3. The Spirit leads us into Christ's future with glad and generous hearts.

You can see below how the sets of singing and artwork integrated these emphases.

To assist the participants in embracing these themes, moments of spoken dialogue were interspersed. These four moments of commentary were each recorded by different people with distinct voices and perspectives. Each set included quotes and excerpts of writers from throughout the centuries. Of course, different themes and texts, perhaps spoken live by members of your community, may be substituted. The texts used in Atlanta, as well as the music graphics, are available for your use in crafting a local program, if desired; they are found on the CD-ROM that accompanies this book.

Another goal was to include representative music from many lands where Lutherans are present and active in their cultures with a forward-looking perspective—the church always reforming—rather than focusing on our church's roots in sixteenth-century Germany. You may recognize songs from Germany, Scandinavia, Asia, Latin America, Africa, and America in very diverse musical styles.

Use whatever musicians are available to lead the singing. In Atlanta we were blessed with a team of musicians as diverse as the music itself yet gathered to share one another's songs. Such diverse leadership may not be available everywhere. Local planners are encouraged to use the musical leadership available to them while expanding their vision of who might help lead. Think outside the box; juxtapose musicians who might not normally work together—the results may surprise and delight you!

Different hymns and songs may be substituted while keeping the same thematic flow. Extensive suggestions and helps are available on the CD-ROM.

The Spirit gathers the church . . .
- Jesu, tawa pano/Jesus, we are gathered (ELW 529 and *This Far by Faith* [TFF] 140)
- Mirad cuán bueno (*Libro de liturgia y cántico* [LLC] 475)
- Gather Us In (ELW 532)
- Built on a rock (ELW 652)

. . . around word and sacrament.
- O blessed spring (ELW 447)
- Taste and see (ELW 493 and TFF 126)
- A mighty fortress is our God (ELW 503, 504)

God hears our cries for mercy . . .
- Come now, O Prince of peace (ELW 247)
- Give Us Clean Hands (CCLI Song Number 2060208)
- I Will Rejoice (TFF 271)

. . . and pours out abundant grace.
- Amazing grace (ELW 779)

The Spirit leads us into Christ's future . . .
- The Church (CCLI Song Number 5713181)
- Tú diste a Israel/Una nueva comunidad en Cristo/A New Community in Christ (LLC 476)
- Ubi caritas et amor/Where true charity and love abide (ELW 653)

...with glad and generous hearts.
- Now thank we all our God (ELW 840)
- Gracious Spirit, heed our pleading (ELW 401 and TFF 103)

We also wished to include a visually artistic element to the singing. In Atlanta this was done through a series of projected artworks—one piece per song—presented on a loop highlighting different elements of the painting. Visual artwork accompanying the singing was equally diverse.

The Blind Singer (El cantor ciego)
Francisco de Goya y Lucientes, 1824–1828
Matched with the song "Gather Us In"

The Denial of Saint Peter
Michelangelo Merisi da Caravaggio, c. 1610
Matched with the song "Built on a rock"

Women at the Tomb of Christ
Syrian well painting, artist unknown, 3rd century
Matched with the song "O blessed spring"

The Crucifixion
Lucas Cranach the Elder, 1502
Matched with the song "Taste and See"

A Mighty Fortress
Mary Button, 2015
Matched with the song "A mighty fortress is our God"

Messiah
He Qi, 2014
Matched with the song "Come now, O Prince of peace"

Simon of Cyrene Helps Jesus Carry the Cross
Mary Button, 2014
Matched with the song "Give Us Clean Hands"

Wisdom
Unknown German source, c. 1170
Matched with the song "I Will Rejoice"

Return of the Prodigal Son
Rembrandt van Rijn, 1636
Matched with the song "Amazing grace"

Flower Beds in Holland
Vincent van Gogh, c. 1883
Matched with the song "The Church"

Christ Asleep during the Tempest
Eugène Delacroix, c. 1853
Matched with the song "Tú diste a Israel"

Jesus Washes Peter's Feet
Unknown Ethiopian
Matched with the song "Ubi caritas et amor"

Spanish Fountain
John Singer Sargent, 1912
Matched with the song "Now thank we all our God"

Electronic files of this artwork are available on the CD-ROM that accompanies this book. Different art may be substituted while keeping the same thematic flow and even the same songs. Perhaps local artists could be utilized with live art, rather than projected. Dance, drama, poetry, and other forms are all possible as well.

Note: Be sure that appropriate copyright permission is obtained if reprinting music into a folder for use by the assembly or if using the artwork suggested. Some music and artwork may be in the public domain while other pieces require permission. Information to assist you in obtaining permission is included in the document on the CD-ROM. Permission guidelines for image use can be found on p.189 of this volume.

The community gathered in Atlanta for the first experience of this journey was unique. We came together for only a few days, representing worshiping communities from across the whole church with all our different musical vocabularies, resources, histories, and pieties. Those who plan to recreate this journey during the 2017 anniversary will represent different communities. Some may decide to use the songs, art, and commentary exactly as presented in Atlanta. Others may customize the program for their particular context. Perhaps some will add additional parts for choirs and brass. Others may simplify for use with more modest musical resources. Some may have the commentaries spoken by a person present, while others may use the video clips provided. Some may choose to substitute different hymns or songs. Some may use the artwork files as they are presented, even when substitute songs are sung. Some may choose not to use the artwork at all and to use local art instead. Some may choose to enhance with additional arts, such as dance, drama, poetry, and photography. The possibilities are plentiful.

We encourage you to explore the extensive resources on the CD-ROM about "The Church's Journey." Use this information to spark your own imagination. It includes an extensive compilation of alternative hymns and songs that adhere closely to the themes of the original choices; the text of the commentaries, if it is desired to have this spoken live rather than using the video clips; source information for related instrumental parts, concertato or stanza settings; and so forth.

Whether local planners craft an event that is similar to the core plan or use alternate music, artwork, and commentary, we hope that any commemoration of the 500th anniversary of the Reformation through music and art is grounded in our tradition, expresses the church broadly, and is honest and always looking forward.

BLESSINGS AND PRAYERS BASED ON THOSE IN LUTHER'S SMALL CATECHISM

The Small Catechism of Martin Luther includes blessings for morning, evening, and around the household meal. These prayers are a treasured heritage and deservedly continue to be widely used. In the spirit of Luther's original blessings, these alternatives are offered—not to replace those by Luther, but to supplement them. These new versions are written with today's Christians in mind and in some cases are designed for particular situations. Luther's originals may be found in *Evangelical Lutheran Worship*, pages 1166–67. For marking baptismal anniversaries, we commend *Let the Children Come: A Baptism Manual for Parents and Sponsors* by Daniel Erlander, pages 29–30.

TABLE BLESSINGS

A Table Blessing to Begin a Meal for Families

One of the family speaks this or another similar Bible passage.
The earth is the LORD's and all that is in it,
the world, and those who live in it. (Ps. 24:1 NRSV)

Then all who are able speak this prayer together.
All here gathered, food from the land,
all is gift from your gracious hand.
Feed us today; feed all those who hunger;
teach us to feed one another.
We ask this in the name of the one who is our bread, Jesus Christ. Amen.

A Table Blessing to End a Meal for Families

One of the family speaks this or another similar Bible passage.
Rejoice in the Lord always. (Phil. 4:4)

Then this prayer is spoken. All may speak it together, or it may be said responsively between one and all as indicated.
For our food, **we rejoice.**
For our friends, **we rejoice.**
For every good gift, **we rejoice.**
Thank you, O God, for this time to eat together.
In Jesus' name we pray. **Amen.**

A Table Blessing for a Group Gathering

Blessed are you, O God, giver of all.
You adorn our tables with food and give companionship for our journeys.
Be present with us as we are fed in body and spirit,
that our sharing this meal is a sign of your life broken and shared for the world.
In Jesus' name we pray. Amen.

A Table Blessing to End a Meal

Blessed are you, O God, giver of all.
We give you thanks for this food that nourishes us.
We give you thanks for this good earth that provides for us and for all your creatures.
Open our hands in humble service to the land and its people.
In Jesus' name we pray. Amen.

A Blessing for Those Who Eat Alone

You have been gracious to your land, O LORD. (Ps. 85:1 ELW)

Gracious God, you are the source of all goodness.
For this food before me, thank you.
For the hands that prepared it, thank you.
For the lands and water that provide nourishment, thank you.
Extend my offering of thanks through works of justice, peace, and love
for the earth and all its creatures.
In the name of Jesus. Amen.

DAILY PRAYERS
Morning Blessing

You may make the sign of the cross.

I am a beloved child of God, marked with the cross of Christ forever.

Your mercies are new every morning. (Based on Lam. 3:23)

Thank you, gracious God, for the gift of this new day.
Awaken me to your abiding presence;
open my eyes to your creation;
open my ears to your promises;
open my heart to the needs of others.
Fill me with your Spirit and guide me this day
in works of kindness, justice, and mercy.
I ask this in the name of Jesus, the light and life of the world. Amen.

Evening Blessing

You may make the sign of the cross.

I am a beloved child of God, marked with the cross of Christ forever.

Come to me, all you that are weary . . . and I will give you rest. (Matt. 11:28)

Thank you, gracious God, for the gift of this coming night.
Restore me with your right spirit.
Calm my mind.
Quiet my heart.
Enfold me with your bountiful mercy.
Protect me from all harm, that I sleep assured of the peace found in you alone.
I ask this in the name of Jesus, who gives us rest. Amen.

A Prayer to Begin the Work Day

May the graciousness of the Lord our God be upon us; prosper the work of our hands. (Ps. 90:17 ELW)

Generous God, you call us to lives of service.
In my words and actions this day, move me to serve in Christ's name.
When I lack energy, inspire me.
When I lack courage, strengthen me.
When I lack compassion, be merciful to me.

You may make the sign of the cross.

In all things, O God, you are our way, our truth, and our life.
Reveal through me your life-giving work, that I love my neighbors as myself.
I ask this in Jesus' name. Amen.

A Prayer to Begin the School Day

Show me your ways, O LORD, and teach me your paths. (Ps. 25:4 ELW)

A prayer based on the Prayer of St. Patrick:

Christ be with me: in you I am never alone.
Christ within me: your Spirit is at work in me.
Christ behind me: reassure me when I struggle.
Christ before me: lead me when I am uncertain.
Christ beneath me: support me when I am weak.
Christ above me: encourage me to do my best.
Christ in quiet: I listen for the sound of your voice.
Christ in danger: I will not fear, for you are with me.

You may make the sign of the cross.

In all things, O God, you are our way, our truth, and our life.
Teach me to love you and my neighbors as myself.
I ask this in Jesus' name. Amen.

Jennifer Baker-Trinity

READ, MARK, AND LEARN

CELEBRATING AND LEARNING
—the Reformation for Children and Adults

The Reformation happened a long time ago—500 years in 2017, to be exact. So even though it was an important event, many people these days are fuzzy, at best, on the details. How do we help them get up to speed on Martin and Katie Luther, indulgences, theses, the Diet of Worms (!), and all the rest?

We suggest you begin with a graphic novel. If you aren't familiar with those, you might recognize it as a comic book, in the broadest sense. Augsburg Fortress has a graphic novel (available August 2016) called *Papa Luther*. It tells the story of Martin Luther through his conversations with his children. Along the way, we learn about his strict upbringing, his life as a monk, his conflicts with pope and emperor over indulgences, and much more. Luther's children, especially Hans and Magda, are central characters, and just the ages of the 8-to-13-year-olds this is geared toward. But the story is dramatic and presented in full color, so we think this resource will appeal to many outside that age range.

For adults who want more detail, and might like a book they can keep around to remember this major anniversary, we lift up *Together by Grace*, a book that tells not only about Luther and the Reformation, but the exciting ventures Lutherans are involved in around the world to this very day. It is written by some of the top teachers and leaders in the church and presented in a colorful format. This book, too, will be available in August 2016.

Study guides for both these resources will be available online. For more information, see "For Further Exploration" on page 177 of this sourcebook, or go to augsburgfortress.org.

REFORMATION FAIR

Looking for still more? Maybe something involving everyone—children and adults—in experiential learning, something fun? How about something like a Reformation Fair!

Those who buy *Papa Luther,* the new graphic novel for children and others, will learn that market day was a big deal in Wittenberg and other German towns. Farmers and artisans would be selling their wares to those who needed them, and it provided a time for everyone to mingle, to find out what was going on, maybe even to hear about the bold ideas of a young professor at the university. And when it was time for a larger celebration, it was even more exciting.

So, for this one day, why not put regular educational offerings on hold, and put your energies into one great gathering for members, visitors, all who come? You could call it a Reformation Fair, or if you prefer German, *Reformationsmesse.* It would be intergenerational, everyone mingling together. There would be activities for all ages, with the older ones helping the younger. If you have a large auditorium, it could be set up in there; otherwise, classrooms could each hold one or more activities. You might want to print a map showing where the various centers are to be found. People could be given a "passport" that could be stamped or punched at each station.

What sorts of activities could be included? Here are some starter ideas; for more, follow Augsburg Fortress on Pinterest and explore the Reformation Fair board.

- Think beyond simple coloring sheets or word puzzles to collaborative art or craft projects—especially if they might be used to enhance worship.
- Luther's rose is a well-known symbol. How might it be rendered creatively? Perhaps in a pointillist manner (many small dots), or with Legos, or in a three-dimensional fashion, using a Rainbow Loom or clay.
- Find or fashion a door (the larger it is, the more impact) and set it up in a sturdy way so that nails (95 of them?) can be pounded into it. Explain that according to tradition, this is how Luther invited discussion about his thoughts.
- Set up a photo booth with props for Martin and Katie Luther.
- Have a small stage where actors (with audience participation and a lot of fun) can act out key scenes from Luther's life, such as:
  - Him being caught in a thunderstorm and vowing to become a monk
  - Posting of the 95 Theses. (For comic effect and for accuracy, include him putting them in an envelope and mailing them to his bishop.)
  - His bold confession at the Diet of Worms
  - His being kidnapped by friendly bandits afterward
  - Katie and other nuns being smuggled out of their convent in a wagon full of pickle barrels
  - The Luther family and others singing hymns like "A mighty fortress" or "From heaven above"
- Create a printing press (using potatoes or linoleum blocks) to compare with copying by hand. You could use a simple phrase like "Here I stand."
- Have an indulgence-selling booth where it's made clear that, finally, you don't need to pay a thing for God's love and forgiveness.
- Since Luther wrote many books, a station could be for assembling and decorating a Little Free Library (see littlefreelibrary.org).
- Create a game show station, perhaps in the style of Jeopardy. PowerPoint templates are available on the web. Use trivia about the Reformation, with answers from easy to harder—compete in teams.
- Have a setting where an adult or teen reads *Papa Luther* to younger children.
- An often-overlooked facet of the Reformation was the establishment of a community chest, gathering money for the welfare of poorer people, including their education. Create a "chest," and invite people to drop in money for an announced cause.
- Food! Think of fun food and drink to evoke Reformation times. Beer (root beer) is important, since the water wasn't safe to drink. Pretzels are a German food whose shape reminds us of arms crossed in prayer.

STUDIES BY AND FOR LUTHERANS AND ROMAN CATHOLICS
Introduction to Lutheran–Catholic Documents

Participants in the events of Reformation 500 will notice that "celebration" is not the first word used for this anniversary. This practice follows from the commitment that unlike earlier centenary anniversary years, 2017 will thankfully be a time to claim the advances in ecumenical relations, especially in Lutheran–Catholic relations, over the last half-century. Thus the Lutheran World Federation (LWF) identified "ecumenical" as one of three defining principles of this year. To an amazing degree, what began as a resolve not to re-inflame wounds of Christian division has become an opportunity to move forward toward greater unity. The implications of this approach will be evident to the world on October 31, 2016, when Pope Francis joins with Lutheran leaders to inaugurate the 500th anniversary year at a service in Lund Cathedral in Sweden.

To understand how the pope can be leading worship to commemorate the Reformation it is helpful to consider a number of texts that explore the steps which have brought Lutherans and Catholics to this new point. These documents invite the imaginations of readers from diverse contexts to ask what further steps are now both possible and necessary in their own settings in order to build upon these new perspectives.

1. THE "FROM CONFLICT TO COMMUNION" CLUSTER

Here it is easiest to work backwards in time, beginning with the newest of the three texts sharing this name:

- *Common Prayer: From Conflict to Communion* (see pages 51-74 in this sourcebook) is the liturgy for the ecumenical commemoration in Lund on October 31, 2016—but the order of service is deliberately intended also for adaptation and use in local settings. It would be a good resource for planning ecumenical worship in many places. As the introduction says, "In this particular and unique ecumenical commemoration, thanksgiving and lament, joy and repentance, mark the singing and the praying as we commemorate the gifts of the Reformation and ask forgiveness for the division that we have perpetuated; [these] . . . lead us to common witness and commitment to each other and for the world."
- *Study Guide: From Conflict to Communion* was produced by an ELCA–Catholic collaboration in Pennsylvania to commend the original *From Conflict to Communion*. An inviting

discussion-starter, it approaches its target text by beginning where that document concluded, with "Five Ecumenical Imperatives." At each step, the Study Guide identifies key paragraphs from the work of the dialogue and connects them with experiences and questions likely to occur in any discussion setting. Suitable for use in single congregations but ideal in ecumenically diverse groups, this study guide does not assume formal theological background or an ecumenical vocabulary. It deftly "guides" the study of the dialogue text so that those who follow its course will have learned a great deal—about the Reformation, about their own churches, and about their personal encounters with painful separation and their longings for growth in unity.

· *From Conflict to Communion: Lutheran–Catholic Common Commemoration of the Reformation in 2017*, the substantial study text giving the title to the two other documents, is a 2012 report of the international Lutheran–Roman Catholic Commission on Unity, appointed by the LWF and the Vatican's Pontifical Council for Promoting Christian Unity.

The chapters first survey the broad changes which allow 2017 to be the "first ecumenical commemoration of the Reformation" and then provide deep soundings into the work which supports this new tone. Drawing on "new perspectives on Martin Luther and on the Reformation," the report outlines major themes in Luther's theology in accessible and authoritative ways that will provide new insights to those at all levels of previous acquaintance with the Reformer. Recognizing that a common telling of a combative history is itself a healing act, the report goes a long way toward such a shared account of how Lutherans and Catholics diverged—and of how the dialogues of the last 50 years have begun to address their theological divisions.

The text repays careful attention. It was written with the hope of a wide audience of serious readers—but those who don't typically read theology at bedtime may want to approach it through the Study Guide.

2. DECLARATION ON THE WAY: CHURCH, MINISTRY, AND EUCHARIST

This is a pioneering form of ecumenical statement. Unlike *From Conflict to Communion*, it is not the report of a single dialogue. Instead, it seeks to harvest the results of fifty years of dialogues at both international and also national or regional levels, and to offer them to be taken into the lives of our church communities. Its focus is on three crucial topics: church, ministry, and eucharist. Its discovery is that, even on these very complicated issues where there has been much discouragement, there is more agreement than most of us had realized.

To be sure, on these areas Lutherans and Catholics have not arrived—they are "on the way." But they are indeed on the way. They are already in "real if imperfect communion" with one another; mutual recognition of ministries is not all or nothing; common affirmations about the eucharist are considerable. Communion between these ecclesial traditions is still painfully imperfect, but it is real. The *Declaration* asks Lutherans and Catholics to claim how far they have come in order to strengthen their resolve to continue further. On the book's cover is noted Chinese artist He Qi's painting of disciples walking on the road to Emmaus—an evocative image for this moment of relationship.

Like *From Conflict to Communion*, this document can be read at different levels of intensity. For a first encounter, this outline may help:

- The Preface and Introduction provide a useful overview.
- Chapter II, the Statement of Agreements, is the heart of the document. These statements are affirmations on church, ministry, and eucharist that Lutherans and Catholics in dialogue have already made together.
- Chapter III is the most directed to specialist readers. It provides supporting evidence for the agreements and thus is most easily skimmed or saved for a second reading.
- Chapter IV treats some remaining differences, of varying seriousness. Most readers will want at least to sample what these issues include.
- The Conclusion, "Next Steps on the Way," focuses on possible actions that are immediately possible and on future implications. As with *From Conflict to Communion*, this can provide both a starting point and the final topic for group discussion. Responses are invited to be locally appropriate, diverse, and bold.

At the 2016 ELCA Churchwide Assembly, the Declaration is on the agenda. If the action to "receive the thirty-two Statements of Agreement" is approved, then the ELCA will be recognizing that, as the Declaration says, between Lutherans and Catholics "there are no longer church-dividing issues with respect to these statements." The action will commend not only the *Declaration on the Way* but also *From Conflict to Communion* and the [1999] *Joint Declaration on the Doctrine of Justification* as "resources for the common life of the church as we approach 2017 and beyond."

Whatever the ELCA decides on this specific proposal, Lutherans and Catholics will not return to past mutual condemnations and animosities. As the LWF has declared, "Lutheran reformation today is about responding together with Christians of other church traditions to the calling of Jesus Christ."

3. *ONE HOPE: RE-MEMBERING THE BODY OF CHRIST*

Note also that an additional, unofficial resource called *One Hope: Re-Membering the Body of Christ*, is available from Augsburg Fortress and Liturgical Press. The work of three Roman Catholic and three Lutheran writers who engaged in a week of conversation and collaboration to prepare this book, it describes in practical ways the dimensions of unity that already exist, and it is suitable for use in congregational and ecumenical study.

For details on how to access the documents mentioned here, see "For Further Exploration," page 177 in this sourcebook.

Kathryn Johnson

COMMEMORATING 1517 WITHOUT DRESSING UP AS LUTHER WITH A HAMMER

How might we best observe the 500th anniversary of the events of 1517, the beginnings of the Western Christian Reformation? I will organize my comments by delineating two quite different ways to understand what this occasion might be all about: Lutherans celebrating Luther, or Lutherans and Roman Catholics together commemorating our common Christian past, our shared present, and a future of hope.

LUTHERANS CELEBRATING LUTHER

One interpretative proposal for 2017 that might overload cyberspace is that Lutherans are to use this time to celebrate the achievements of Martin Luther. I foresee a parish member dressed up as Luther carrying a hammer and joining the Sunday morning's liturgical procession or the pastor dressed as a friar and waving his hammer in the pulpit. Let me urge caution about this plan. I fear that any such staging will embody exaggerated and inaccurate historical fragments and may serve to reinforce out-of-date prejudices.

Persons who are contemplating this option need to be made aware of the following:
- that much of what is popularly believed and taught about the events of 1517 is historically inaccurate;
- that Reformation historians are telling us that perhaps Luther only posted, that is, sent in the mail to his bishop, the Ninety-Five Theses, rather than affixing them to any church door;
- that if he did post them on a public bulletin board (or church door), he used wax, not nails;
- that during the early years of the Reformation, the Ninety-Five Theses were never translated into German for the general population to read;
- that the earliest artistic image of Luther with a hammer in his hand appeared in the mid-nineteenth century, a time of militant antagonism between Lutherans and Roman Catholics;
- that the Lutheran comic book I was given as a child, which showed the monastic library as having chained up the Bible to keep it from the people, totally misrepresented the intention of the medieval church to keep rare and valuable Bibles safely available to those who could read.

Despite all this, I note with regret that materials being currently published for 2017 feature Luther and an often-huge hammer as cover art. (Am I the only one for whom "hammer" has negative connotations?) So please do not dress up as Luther with a hammer.

As you hope to educate your congregation about the Reformation, I am sorry to report that each of the several films based on the life of Luther is more or less inadequate or untrustworthy. For example, *Martin Luther, Heretic* (1983), available on YouTube, shows the people of Wittenberg avidly reading the Latin Ninety-Five Theses hot off the press, which they did not. Despite Luther's decades of effort studying, translating, teaching, and preaching the Bible, the films include distressingly few scenes of Luther doing anything with the scriptures. In the worship service portrayed in the 2003 film *Luther*, worshipers are sitting, men and women side by side, in pews with backs, as Luther wanders up and down the aisle while preaching in a casual tone of voice, a depiction inaccurate in every way. I am sorry that these opportunities to convey to contemporary audiences the essence of 1517 are flawed. It is not surprising, however, that each film does feature the hammer.

I judge that the most responsible depictions of Martin Luther show him wearing his doctoral robe as befitting his role as a university professor of biblical studies, and my favorite of all is the Playmobil figure in which a smiling Luther is holding out both the vernacular Bible (Old and New Testaments) and his quill pen. Not a hammer, but the Bible.

To those Lutherans who think a reconstruction of Luther's proposals of orders of worship would be a good idea, my advice is that constructing worship as costume drama is never a good idea. We are to worship God as we are, in our time and place. Indeed, during the twentieth century, liturgical leaders in many of the world's churches labored to authorize and popularize patterns of worship that speak the current language, that honor our own cultural attitudes about gender, that celebrate the resurrection with contemporary music and art. Historical playacting at worship makes heartfelt participation in the praise of God difficult, because in such performances we are always watching ourselves be someone other than we are. I recall an ecumenical Thanksgiving Day service at which the ushers, dressed up as Puritans, paced up and down the aisle carrying those ten-foot poles, which four hundred years ago were used to bop parishioners on the head if they were snoozing during the two-hour sermons. But what we encountered in the 1950s was a parody of the past that did not render our Thanksgiving praise more profound. Besides, Martin Luther was a no-nonsense person who would probably be disgusted to see himself impersonated in worship. He would ask, does this song-and-dance drive Christ (in German, *Christum treiben*)? Like the traditional images of John the Baptist, who is always pointing to Christ, Luther points us to Christ, not to himself. And if you hope to repeat Luther's address at the Diet of Worms, please reflect on the fact that for countless Christians around the world today, especially the young ones, the words "Here I stand" will evoke not a line that perhaps Luther spoke in 1520 (or perhaps he did not; historians disagree about this), but rather the song of Elsa the Ice Queen in the film *Frozen*.

To those who are considering using 2017 to celebrate Luther's accomplishments, I suggest the standard order for holy communion as presented in *Evangelical Lutheran Worship*, filled to the brim with Reformation-era hymns. The volume *The Sunday Assembly* (pages 59, 180–87) gives help here. (Hymn numbers are from ELW.)

Opening confession and forgiveness	600	Out of the depths I cry to you
Kyrie	409	Kyrie! God, Father
Hymn of praise	410	All glory be to God on high
Creed	411	We all believe in one true God
Holy, holy, holy	868	Isaiah, in a vision did of old
Lamb of God	357	Lamb of God, pure and sinless

For the hymn of the day, you might choose hymn 505, a reformed translation of "A mighty fortress is our God." For the eucharistic prayer (please remember that Luther's colleague Philipp Melanchthon praised the eucharistic prayer of the Eastern Orthodox Church), you might select either the prayer from the third or fourth century designated in *Evangelical Lutheran Worship* as Form XI (*ELW*, p. 69) or the prayer that the Lutheran scholar Luther Reed first published in 1947, designated as Form I. For the final blessing, Luther preferred the use of the Aaronic benediction (*ELW*, p. 114).

Perhaps the most appropriate date on which to schedule such a service would be February 19, 2017, one day after the commemoration of Luther, which is set annually on the day of his death, February 18. (Incidentally, his last words were not something about a hammer, but "We are beggars, this is true.") A service such as the one here described is not historical playacting. Rather, it employs the most recent Lutheran order of worship and the best vernacular translations of hymns, so that our worship is indeed of our time and place.

Better than plowing through the Ninety-Five Theses, a congregational study group may make more fruitful use of its time by reading through Luther's "Sermon on Indulgences and Grace" (*The Annotated Luther*, Volume 1: *The Roots of Reform* [Minneapolis: Fortress Press, 2015], 60–65). This popular sermon of 1518, which was reprinted in German twenty-five times in two years, had far more effect on the general population than did the academically formulated Latin Theses. An annotated translation of this sermon (also available in a booklet, *Martin Luther's 95 Theses with Introduction, Commentary, and Study Guide* [Minneapolis: Fortress Press, 2015]) will assist your people in understanding the medieval theological categories of Luther's day. It was the printing of this sermon that made Luther a best-selling author. It is humbling to admit that when we commandeer people from the past to serve our contemporary purposes, we often seriously distort the persons they genuinely were. Indeed, the real Luther would shock, even distress, many of us. This sermon may surprise you with both what sounds familiar and what sounds quite alien to our ears.

LUTHERANS AND ROMAN CATHOLICS PRAYING TOGETHER

I now describe my preferred option: that Lutherans use 2017 not primarily to celebrate Luther, but rather to commemorate, with Lutherans and Roman Catholics together, our common understanding of the past, our collaboration in the present, and our hopes for the future. I hope we Lutherans can worship throughout 2017 as the time that it is: a time of international ecumenical conversation between Lutherans and Roman Catholics, a time of joint resolve to erase errors and to design collaborative projects. Recall that in 1999 the dialogue between Lutherans and Roman Catholics released the *Joint Declaration on the Doctrine of Justification*, which stated that the differing denominational emphases did not invalidate the commonalities between the churches on this central theological issue. This Declaration is available as a PDF file online (http://bit.ly/1QtQEa8). It is a time to forgive each other for past offenses, to rejoice in our common baptism, and to walk together into God's future.

I heard once about a high school in the United States in which students, when studying the American Revolution, used a textbook written and published in Britain. We can emulate this creative approach to our continuing education by reviewing the past with each other's eyes. We can collaborate when recalling history, rather than repeating one-sided and ill-informed memories. We can stand with the countless homes in which one parent is Lutheran and one Roman Catholic, helping these ecumenical households be fervently Christian. We can be grateful that each church body has learned so much from the other. We Lutherans in the Evangelical Lutheran Church in America are no longer worshiping like the villagers in *Babette's Feast*, with one man in a black robe up there talking on and on, but we gladly don historic eucharistic vestments for weekly communion, we sign up to serve as assisting ministers, our assemblies are enriched by the three-year lectionary that was developed in an ecumenical council largely by Roman Catholics. And we rejoice that across the street, Roman Catholics, with their renewed papacy, are faithfully proclaiming God's mercy in three readings each week, with their assembly singing hymns from the past and present, all the baptized knowing that the church is the whole people of God. Our ecclesial communities can stand side by side, enriched by each other's presence, strengthened by each other's voices.

The primary resource for such an understanding of 2017 is the booklet *From Conflict to Communion*, a report prepared for a Lutheran–Catholic common commemoration of 1517 (Report of the Lutheran–Roman Catholic Commission on Unity, Leipzig: Bonifatius, 2013). Both the booklet itself (http://bit.ly/1m8WSRQ) and a helpful study guide (http://bit.ly/1OgoOtG) are available as online PDF files. Jointly prepared by Roman Catholic and Lutheran historians and theologians, this booklet summarizes several centuries of historical events that began in 1517 and that affect both our churches, as well as data describing the twenty-first-century situation of our churches in theology and practice. According to *From Conflict to Communion*, the three contemporary phenomena of ecumenism, globalization, and new evangelization have set us in a radically different place than was that of Luther and Pope Leo X, and this booklet helps us to reexamine our history and to contemplate our actual current situation. No matter how much or how little historical knowledge you and your people have, no matter how attentive you have been to the ecumenical dialogues of the last decades, this booklet will serve you well.

Standing side by side, we can continue to grapple with our theological differences, developing our relationship in new ways, even gently correcting our own and each other's memories. But such conversation is more productive when we can also pray side by side. Please watch your national church's website, www.elca500.org, to see forthcoming 2017 ecumenical worship service suggestions. One such service order is being jointly prepared by the Vatican and the Lutheran World Federation for a joint observance of the anniversary in Lund, Sweden, on October 31, 2016. Also, a spin-off of the commemoration of the Reformation will be held at the May 2017 Lutheran World Federation Assembly in Namibia. Thus some thoughtful worship suggestions will be available for your consideration.

Those of you who are eager to design your own worship service can be inspired by the threefold content of the booklet *From Conflict to Communion*:
- we celebrate the shared joy we have in the gospel;
- we acknowledge the pain over failures and sins and our need for repentance; and
- we pray for the ongoing challenge to bear common witness to Christ throughout the world.

That is: joy, repentance, and common witness. Be sure to balance each Lutheran quote or hymn with one written by a Roman Catholic. If you sing "A mighty fortress is our God," you might also appoint the splendid hymn written in 1983 by the Benedictine sister Delores Dufner, "The Word of God is source and seed" (ELW 506). "What is this place" (ELW 524) by the twentieth-century Roman Catholic Jesuit priest Huub Oosterhuis can be sung next to "Beloved, God's chosen" (ELW 648) by Lutheran laywoman Susan Palo Cherwien. The ninth-century chant "Ubi caritas et amor," "Where True Charity and Love Abide" (ELW 642 or 653), would be a welcome addition, grounding our separate voices in their common past.

You might also pray the beloved seventeenth-century prayer for the church (*ELW*, pp. 58, 73):
> Gracious Father, we pray for your holy catholic church. Fill it with all truth and peace. Where it is corrupt, purify it; where it is in error, direct it; where in anything it is amiss, reform it; where it is right, strengthen it; where it is in need, provide for it; where it is divided, reunite it, for the sake of your Son, Jesus Christ, our Savior.

I smile when I think that this splendid prayer for the church was written by the Anglican archbishop of Canterbury William Laud, who when he was in political power saw to the imprisonment of Puritans and their expulsion from England and then, when tables were turned, was himself executed on the charge of popery. We thank God both that we are no longer in his situation of virulent opposition to other Christians, and that the breadth and depth of Laud's words exceed the narrowness of his personal sense of church. Thus together we can join in his fine prayer.

Perhaps in your location a joint worship service can be cosponsored by your Lutheran church and a local Roman Catholic parish. Perhaps the best scheduling for such an event would be Sunday afternoon, October 29, 2017. It might be difficult to schedule a service on Tuesday evening, October 31, given the American hoopla of Halloween. A committee constituted by people from both denominations could work together on logistics. Perhaps the two parishes can schedule a joint session of Bible study of the texts appointed for the service. As well, the following Sunday will be celebrated in both churches as All Saints Sunday, year A. Thanks to the three-year ecumenical lectionary, the readings in both churches on that Sunday will be from Revelation 7, 1 John 3, and Matthew 5, for also at Sunday morning worship we Lutherans and Roman Catholics are praising God and praying for the world side by side. The ecumenical planning committee might continue to meet, discussing the texts for All Saints Sunday and then later for the upcoming last Sunday of Year A, Christ the King, on which both churches will once again share common readings from Ezekiel 34 and Matthew 25.

I admit that it might be easier to plan congregational events of "rah-rah-Luther" than to collaborate with the Roman Catholics down the street to schedule ecumenical events, especially since many Lutherans may need to be informed about accurate history and the current interchurch situation. Yet using this anniversary to teach about the wider church might honor Luther in a profound way. As the text of *From Conflict to Communion* states, "Because Lutherans believe that they belong to the one body of Christ, Lutherans emphasize that their church did not originate with the Reformation or come into existence only five hundred years ago. Rather, they are convinced that the Lutheran churches have their origin in the Pentecost event and the proclamation of the apostles" (par. 222). And as the document says, "The beginning of the Reformation will be rightly remembered when Lutherans and Catholics hear together the gospel of Jesus Christ and allow themselves to be called anew into community with the Lord" (par. 245). We know that it is not the Lutheran church that saves, but Christ, and our conduct during 2017 gives us the occasion to tell everyone that two once-oppositional communities are now standing side by side, praising God for their common baptism, offering their joint repentance, and committing themselves to an ecumenically informed mission.

God bless your commemoration of 1517.

This essay is based on a presentation given at the ELCA's 2015 Worship Jubilee, "Called to Be a Living Voice."

Gail Ramshaw

THE NINETY-FIVE THESES

In 2017 Lutherans are celebrating the 500th anniversary of the Reformation. Yet the Reformation continued throughout Luther's life and beyond; in fact, we hope it is continuing still today. What happened five hundred years ago, in 1517, was the event that sparked it all: Luther's writing and publicizing of the Ninety-Five Theses.

Most of us have heard of the Ninety-Five Theses, but few of us have read them or even have a clear idea of what they say. And many other writings of Luther are more significant, including his "Sermon on Indulgences and Grace," written to explain his views to nonscholars. Yet the Theses have historical value, and they are reproduced here in a translation by noted Reformation scholar Timothy Wengert.

The best way to read them is in context with a reliable guide. For that reason, Fortress Press has recently published *Martin Luther's 95 Theses* with commentary and introduction by Timothy J. Wengert, and with two accompanying documents by Luther (the October 31, 1517, letter to Archbishop Albrecht and the 1518 *Sermon on Indulgences and Grace*). This short book (978-1-4514-8279-9) includes a study guide and is recommended for both group and individual use. In it you will learn what an indulgence is, how Luther moved from preaching indulgences to preaching against them, and the discussion around whether the Ninety-Five Theses were ever nailed to the church door.

Luther didn't, of course, intend to start a split with the Roman Catholic Church. He merely drew up a list of points for discussion. But those points struck chords that were both theological and nationalistic, were viewed as threatening by the church hierarchy, and the rest is, well, the Reformation!

[THE NINETY-FIVE THESES OR] DISPUTATION FOR CLARIFYING THE POWER OF INDULGENCES

Out of love and zeal for bringing the truth to light, what is written below will be debated in Wittenberg with the Reverend Father Martin Luther, Master of Arts and Sacred Theology and regularly-appointed lecturer on these subjects at that place, presiding. Therefore, he requests that those who cannot be present to discuss orally with us will in their absence do so by letter. In the name of our Lord Jesus Christ. Amen.

1. Our Lord and Master Jesus Christ, in saying "Do penance . . . ," wanted the entire life of the faithful to be one of penitence.

2. This phrase cannot be understood as referring to sacramental Penance, that is, confession and satisfaction as administered by the clergy.

3. Yet it does not mean solely inner penitence—indeed such inner penitence is nothing unless it outwardly produces various mortifications of the flesh.

4. And thus, penalty remains as long as hatred of self (that is, true inner penitence) remains, namely, until our entrance into the kingdom of heaven.

5. Pope neither desires nor is able to remit any penalties except those imposed by his own discretion or that of the canons.

6. The pope cannot remit any guilt except by declaring and confirming its remission by God or, of course, by remitting guilt in [legal] cases reserved to himself. In showing contempt regarding such cases, the guilt would certainly remain.

7. God remits the guilt of absolutely no one unless at the same time God subjects in all things the one humbled to God's vicar, the priest.

8. The penitential canons were imposed only on the living, and, according to the canons themselves, nothing should be imposed on those about to die.

9. Accordingly, the Holy Spirit through the pope acts in a kindly manner toward us in papal decrees by always exempting the moment of death and the case of necessity.

10. Those priests act ignorantly and wickedly who, in the case of the dying, reserve canonical penalties for one's time in purgatory.

11. Those "tares" about changing the canonical penalty into the penalty of purgatory certainly seem to have been "sown" while the bishops "were sleeping."

12. Formerly, canonical penalties were imposed not after, but before absolution, as tests of true contrition.

13. Through death, those about to die are absolved of all [such penalties] and are already dead as far as canon laws are concerned, in that by right they have release from them.

14. Imperfect purity or love on the part of the dying person necessarily brings with it great fear. The smaller the love, the greater the fear.

15. This fear or horror is enough by itself alone (to say nothing of other things) to constitute the penalty of purgatory, since it is very near the horror of despair.

16. It seems that hell, purgatory, and heaven differ from each other as much as despair, near despair, and assurance.

17. It seems necessary that, for souls in purgatory, as the horror decreases so love increases.

18. It neither seems proved—either by any logical arguments or by scripture—that souls in purgatory are outside a state of merit, that is, unable to grow in love;

19. nor does it seem to be proved that these souls, at least not all of them, are certain and assured of their own salvation—even though we ourselves are completely certain about [their destiny].

20. Therefore, the pope understands by the phrase "plenary remission of all penalties" not actually "all penalties" but only "penalties imposed by himself."

21. And so, those indulgence preachers err who say that through the pope's indulgences a person is released and saved from every penalty.

22. On the contrary, to souls in purgatory he remits no penalty that they should have paid in this life according to canon law.

23. If any remission of all penalties whatsoever could be granted to anyone, it would certainly be granted only to the most perfect, that is, to the very fewest.

24. Because of this, most people are inevitably deceived by means of this indiscriminate and high-sounding promise of release from penalty.

25. The kind of power that a pope has over purgatory in general corresponds to the power that any bishop or local priest has in particular in his diocese or parish.

26. The pope does best in that he grants remission to souls [in purgatory] not by "the power of the keys," which he does not possess [here], but "by way of intercession."

27. They "preach human opinions" who say that, as soon as a coin thrown into the money chest clinks, a soul flies out [of purgatory].

28. It is certain that when a coin clinks in the money chest profits and avarice may well be increased, but the intercession of the church rests on God's choice alone.

29. Who knows whether all the souls in purgatory want to be redeemed, given what is recounted about St. Severinus and St. Paschasius?

30. No one is secure in the genuineness of one's own contrition—much less in having attained "plenary remission."

31. As rare as a person who is truly penitent, just so rare is someone who truly acquires indulgences; indeed, the latter is the rarest of all.

32. Those who believe that they can be secure in their salvation through indulgence letters will be eternally damned along with their teachers.

33. One must especially beware of those who say that those indulgences of the pope are "God's inestimable gift" by which a person is reconciled to God.

34. For these indulgent graces are only based upon the penalties of sacramental satisfaction instituted by human beings.

35. Those who teach that contrition is not necessary on the part of those who would rescue souls [from purgatory] or who would buy confessional privileges do not preach Christian views.

36. Any truly remorseful Christian has a right to full remission of guilt and penalty, even without indulgence letters.

37. Any true Christian, living or dead, possesses a God-given share in all the benefits of Christ and the church, even without indulgence letters.

38. Nevertheless, remission and participation [in these benefits] from the pope must by no means be despised, because—as I said—they are the declaration of divine remission.

39. It is extremely difficult, even for the most learned theologians, to lift up before the people the liberality of indulgences and the truth about contrition at one and the same time.

40. The "truth about contrition" seeks and loves penalties [for sins]; the "liberality of indulgences" relaxes penalties and at very least gives occasion for hating them.

41. Apostolic indulgences are to be preached with caution, so that the people do not mistakenly think that they are to be preferred to other good works of love.

42. Christians are to be taught that the pope does not intend the acquiring of indulgences to be compared in any way with works of mercy.

43. Christians are to be taught that the one who gives to a poor person or lends to the needy does a better deed than if a person acquires indulgences,

44. because love grows through works of love and a person is made better; but through indulgences one is not made better but only freer from penalty [for sin].

45. Christians are to be taught that anyone who sees a destitute person and, while passing such a one by, gives money for indulgences does not buy [gracious] indulgences of the pope but God's wrath.

46. Christians are to be taught that, unless they have more than they need, they must set aside enough for their household and by no means squander it on indulgences.

47. Christians are to be taught that buying indulgences is a matter of free choice, not commanded.

48. Christians are to be taught that the pope, while granting indulgences, needs and thus desires their devout prayer for him more than their money.

49. Christians are to be taught that papal indulgences are useful [for them] only if they do not put their trust in them but extremely harmful if they lose their fear of God because of them.

50. Christians are to be taught that if the pope knew the demands made by the indulgence preachers, he would rather that the Basilica of St. Peter were burned to ashes than that it be constructed using the skin, flesh, and bones of his sheep.

51. Christians are to be taught that the pope ought to give and would want to give of his own wealth—even selling the Basilica of St. Peter if necessary—to those from whom certain declaimers of indulgences are wheedling money.

52. It is vain to trust in salvation by means of indulgence letters, even if the [indulgence] agent— or even the pope himself—were to offer his own soul as security for them.

53. People who forbid the preaching of the Word of God in some churches altogether in order that indulgences may be preached in others are enemies of Christ and the pope.

54. An injustice is done to the Word of God when, in the very same sermon, equal or more time is spent on indulgences than on the Word.

55. It is necessarily the pope's intent that if indulgences, which are a completely insignificant thing, are celebrated with one bell, one procession, and one ceremony, then the gospel, which is the greatest thing of all, should be preached with a hundred bells, a hundred processions, and a hundred ceremonies.

56. The treasures of the church, from which the pope distributes indulgences, are not sufficiently discussed or known among Christ's people.

57. That [these treasures] are not transient worldly riches is certainly clear, because many of the [indulgence] declaimers do not so much freely distribute such riches as only collect them.

58. Nor are they the merits of Christ and the saints, because, even without the pope, these merits always work grace for the inner person and cross, death, and hell for the outer person.

59. St. Laurence said that the poor of the church were the treasures of the church, but he spoke according to the usage of the word "treasure" in his own time.

60. Not without cause, we say that the keys of the church (given by the merits of Christ) are that treasure.

61. For it is clear that the pope's power only suffices for the remission of [ecclesiastical] penalties and for [legal] actions.

62. The true treasure of the church is the most holy gospel of the glory and grace of God.

63. But this treasure is deservedly the most hated, because it makes "the first last."

64. In contrast, the treasure of indulgences is deservedly the most acceptable, because it makes "the last first."

65. Therefore, the treasures of the gospel are nets with which they formerly fished for men of wealth.

66. The treasures of indulgences are nets with which they now fish for the wealth of men.

67. Indulgences, which the declaimers shout about as the greatest "graces," are indeed understood as such—insofar as they promote profits.

68. Yet they are in truth the least of all when compared to the grace of God and the goodness of the cross.

69. Bishops and parish priests are bound to admit agents of the Apostolic indulgences with all reverence.

70. But all of them are much more bound to strain eyes and ears intently, so that these [agents] do not preach their own daydreams in place of the pope's commission.

71. Let the one who speaks against the truth of the Apostolic indulgences be anathema and accursed,

72. but let the one who guards against the arbitrary and unbridled words used by declaimers of indulgences be blessed.

73. Just as the pope justly thunders against those who, in whatever way they can, contrive to harm the sale of indulgences,

74. much more so does he intend to thunder against those who, under the pretext of indulgences, contrive to harm holy love and the truth.

75. To imagine that papal indulgences are so great that they could absolve a person even for doing the impossible by violating the mother of God is insanity.

76. On the contrary, we have said that papal indulgences cannot take away the very least of venial sins, as far as guilt is concerned.

77. That it is said that even St. Peter, if he were now pope, could not grant greater graces is blasphemy against St. Peter and the pope.

78. On the contrary, we say that even the present pope, or any pope whatsoever, possesses greater graces—namely, the gospel, "deeds of power, gifts of healing . . ."—as in 1 Cor. 12[:28].

79. To say that the cross, emblazoned with the papal coat-of-arms and erected [in the church where indulgences are preached], is of equal worth to the cross of Christ is blasphemy.

80. The bishops, parish priests, and theologians who allow such sermons free course among the people will have to answer for this.

81. This unbridled preaching makes it difficult even for learned men to defend the reverence due the pope from slander or from the truly sharp questions of the laity:

82. Namely, "Why does the pope not empty purgatory for the sake of the holiest love and the direst need of souls as a matter of the highest justice, given that he redeems countless souls for filthy lucre to build the Basilica [of St. Peter] as a completely trivial matter?"

83. Again, "Why continue funeral and anniversary masses for the dead instead of returning or permitting the withdrawal of the endowments founded for them, since it is against the law to pray for those already redeemed?"

84. Again, "What is this new piety of God and the pope that, for the sake of money, they permit someone who is impious and an enemy to redeem [from purgatory] a pious, God-pleasing soul and yet do not, for the sake of the need of that very pious and beloved soul, redeem it purely out of love?"

85. Again, "Why are the penitential canons—long since abrogated and dead in actual fact and through disuse—nevertheless now bought off with money through granting indulgences, as if they were very much alive?"

86. Again, "Why does the pope, whose riches today are more substantial than the richest Crassus, not simply construct the Basilica of St. Peter with his own money rather than with the money of the poor faithful?"

87. Again, "What exactly does the pope 'remit' or 'allow participation in' when it comes to those who through perfect contrition have a right to full remission and a share [in the church's benefits]?"

88. Again, "Could any greater good come to the church than if the pope were to bestow these remissions and participation to each of the faithful a hundred times a day, as he now does but once?"

89. "Since, rather than money, the pope seeks the salvation of souls through indulgences, why does he now suspend the documents and indulgences previously granted, although they have equal efficacy?"

90. To suppress these very pointed arguments of the laity by force alone and not to resolve them by providing reasons is to expose the church and the pope to ridicule by their enemies and to make Christians miserable.

91. Therefore, if indulgences were preached according to the spirit and intention of the pope, all of these [objections] would be easily resolved—indeed, they would not exist.

92. And thus, away with all those prophets who say to Christ's people, "Peace, peace," and there is no peace!

93. May it go well for all of those prophets who say to Christ's people, "Cross, cross," and there is no cross!

94. Christians must be encouraged diligently to follow Christ, their head, through penalties, death, and hell,

95. and in this way they may be confident of "entering heaven through many tribulations" rather than through the [false] security of peace.

MARTIN LUTHER, THE CATECHISM, AND MUSIC

NOTES FOR THE LEADER

You may choose to study all five hymns as a single lesson, study each hymn with the corresponding part of the Small Catechism, or use some but not all of the hymn studies.

RESOURCES

Each participant should have access to a copy of *Evangelical Lutheran Worship*. Luther's Small Catechism is included in ELW beginning on page 1160. Participants will also need access to a Bible for one of the questions about Luther's baptismal hymn.

Copies of this lesson can be distributed to the participants, or a leader can simply walk the participants through the discussion of each hymn.

Reproducible public-domain texts are provided as part of this study for two catechism hymns that are not included in *Evangelical Lutheran Worship*. For those who prefer to view the hymn texts online rather than to print copies, the following web links were valid as of March 2016:

Text of Luther's Ten Commandments hymn: http://www.projectwittenberg.org/pub/resources/text/wittenberg/hymns/godlylife.txt and at http://nethymnal.org/htm/t/h/thatmana.htm (with a music file).

Text of Luther's baptism hymn: http://openhymnal.org/Lyrics/To_Jordan_Came_Our_Lord_The_Christ-Christ_Unser_Herr.html and at http://nethymnal.org/htm/t/j/c/tjctcolo.htm (with a music file).

A NOTE ABOUT LANGUAGE

Please note that the language of the translations that are in the public domain is often dated. This may pose a challenge to students, but it is also an opportunity to talk about the importance of Luther's work as a translator. Translation isn't just about different languages like Latin, German, and English. Effective translation requires using language that regular people can understand. Because language changes over time, it is important for the church to follow Luther's example of retranslating the scriptures, liturgy, and hymns, as well as writing new hymns, to communicate the Christian faith clearly in new contexts.

Kathryn A. Kleinhans

Martin Luther, the Catechism, and Music

A LESSON FOR CONFIRMANDS OF ALL AGES

Have you ever noticed how much easier it is to remember words that have been set to music? Martin Luther realized this too. He wrote many hymns to make it easier for Christians to learn about their faith. Sometimes he wrote new words for a familiar tune. Sometimes he took a hymn he had already written and set the words to a new and more memorable tune. Studying Luther's catechism hymns may help you learn and remember too!

Luther's Ten Commandments Hymn

"These Are the Holy Ten Commands"; alternate title: "That Man a Godly Life Might Live"

1. If you were going to write a hymn to teach people the Ten Commandments, how many stanzas would you write?

2. Now look at Luther's Ten Commandments hymn. How many verses did he write?

3. Which verses can be matched up with actual commandments?

4. Which verses are Luther's commentary about the Ten Commandments?

5. In stanzas 1 and 11, Luther explains why God gave us the Ten Commandments. What reason does Luther give in stanza 1? What reasons does Luther give in stanza 11? What is the difference between the reasons given in these two stanzas?

6. Luther ends every stanza of this hymn with the same words. What are they? Why do you think he repeats these words?

7. Commands are a form of speech that tell someone to do something. The final stanza of Luther's Ten Commandments hymn is a different form of speech. Who is being addressed, and why? What do we call this kind of speech? Why do you think Luther chose to end his hymn this way?

Luther's Apostles' Creed Hymn

WE ALL BELIEVE IN ONE TRUE GOD (ELW 411)

Open your hymnal to the Apostles' Creed on page 105. Put a bookmark there and a bookmark at ELW 411 so you can go back and forth between the creed and the hymn.

1. Read the first article of the creed aloud together. Now read the first stanza of Luther's hymn. How does Luther describe God's activity as Creator?

   How does Luther describe God's activity as a parent?

   How are these two activities (creating and parenting) related?

2. Read the second article of the creed aloud together. Now read the second stanza of Luther's hymn. What words or images stand out for you?
   What phrases from the creed does Luther leave out of this stanza? Does Luther add anything?

   In this part of the hymn, Luther refers to Jesus as "our elder brother." What does it mean to you to think of Jesus as "our elder brother"? As *your* elder brother?

   Luther describes Jesus both as God's Son and as our brother. What does that say about us? About you?

3. Read the third article of the creed aloud together. Now read the third stanza of Luther's hymn. The third article of the creed lists a series of important Christian beliefs. What verbs does Luther use to describe the things listed in the creed?

   Why do you think it was important for Luther to describe the relationship between the things in the third article of the creed instead of just listing them?

Luther's Lord's Prayer Hymn

OUR FATHER, GOD IN HEAVEN ABOVE (ELW 747)

1. What do you think the purpose of prayer is? How do you feel about prayer?

2. Compare the first stanza of Luther's Lord's Prayer hymn with Luther's explanation to the beginning of the Lord's Prayer in the Small Catechism (*ELW*, p. 1163). How does Luther describe the purpose of prayer? What kinds of feelings does Luther associate with prayer?

3. Many of the petitions of the Lord's Prayer ask God to act in certain ways. In the second stanza, Luther's hymn asks God to help us act in certain ways. Why do you think he does that?

4. Read the first sentence of Luther's explanations to the first, second, and third petitions of the Lord's Prayer in the Small Catechism (the first sentence answers the question "What is this?"). Pay attention to the last half of each sentence, especially the very last word. What do you think about the way Luther shifts the focus of the Lord's Prayer from God to us? Where do you see this shift in focus in the hymn?

5. In the fifth stanza, Luther describes "daily bread" broadly, including many other things we need for our daily life besides food. What sense does it make to you to think of things like defense and peace as part of our daily bread? Are there things you would add to Luther's list? How do we identify what we really need in life, not just what we want?

6. In stanzas 7 and 8, Luther refers to "time of trial" and "fearsome days." Where do we experience trials and temptations in our lives? What causes us (you!) to be afraid? How might prayer help us respond to our trials, our temptations, and our fears?

7. Read the final stanza of the hymn. Sometimes we think of *Amen* as nothing more than a way of saying "The end," but Luther devotes an entire stanza to it. What does he tell us that *Amen* means? What new insights does this stanza give you about the purpose of prayer and about what we should expect when we pray?

Luther's Baptism Hymn

TO JORDAN CAME THE CHRIST, OUR LORD

1. In the first stanza, how does Luther describe the purpose of Jesus' baptism? How does he describe the purpose of our baptism?

2. In stanzas 3 and 4, how does Luther relate Jesus' baptism to our own baptism?

3. In this hymn, as in the Small Catechism, Luther makes the point that baptism is not just water. What does he connect water with in stanza 2? What does he connect water with in stanza 7?

4. In the Small Catechism, what benefits does Luther say that baptism gives (*ELW*, p. 1165)? Where do you see these benefits in Luther's hymn?

5. Read stanza 5 of Luther's hymn, and then read these short Bible passages: Matthew 28:18-20; Mark 16:15-16; and John 3:3-5, 16-17. How do you see the themes of these Bible passages reflected in Luther's hymn?

6. Close your eyes and listen to someone read the final stanza of the hymn aloud. What words or images stand out for you as you listen?

Luther's Communion Hymn

O LORD, WE PRAISE YOU (ELW 499)

The first stanza of this hymn dates from the fifteenth century, before the Reformation. Luther liked it because it was a song people sang during communion. He added two more stanzas to the hymn, emphasizing his understanding of communion as God's gift.

1. What verbs does Luther use in the hymn to describe *God's* action in the sacrament of communion? What verbs does Luther use to describe *our* action?

2. Before the Reformation, it was not common for people to receive communion more than once a year. Often, when they attended the service, they simply watched the priest's actions and did not participate. Look through Luther's hymn for words emphasizing our participation in communion. Why do you think Luther uses words like *feast* and *banquet* in this hymn? What feelings or actions is he trying to evoke?

3. In the Small Catechism, what benefits does Luther say communion gives (*ELW*, p. 1166)? Where do you see these benefits in Luther's hymn?

4. "O Lord, have mercy!" is sung twice in each of the three stanzas of the hymn. When and where are the words "Lord, have mercy" sung in our worship service? What are the words a response to, in the liturgy and in this hymn?

5. Luther also ended every stanza of his Ten Commandments hymn with the words, "Have mercy, Lord." Do the words sound or feel different when used in these two different hymns? Where in our world, or in your own life, is God's mercy most needed?

That Man a Godly Life Might Live

1. That man a godly life might live,
   God did these ten commandments give
   by his true servant Moses, high
   upon the Mount Sinai.
   Have mercy, Lord!

2. I am thy God and Lord alone,
   no other God beside me own;
   put thy whole confidence in me
   and love me e'er cordially.
   Have mercy, Lord!

3. By idle word and speech profane
   take not my holy name in vain
   and praise but that as good and true
   which I myself say and do.
   Have mercy, Lord!

4. Hallow the day which God hath blest
   that thou and all thy house may rest;
   keep hand and heart from labor free
   that God may so work in thee.
   Have mercy, Lord!

5. Give to thy parents honor due,
   be dutiful, and loving, too,
   and help them when their strength decays,
   so shalt thou have length of days.
   Have mercy, Lord!

6. In sinful wrath thou shalt not kill
   nor hate nor render ill for ill;
   be patient and of gentle mood,
   and to thy foe do thou good.
   Have mercy, Lord!

7. Be faithful to thy marriage vows,
   thy heart give only to thy spouse;
   thy life keep pure, and lest thou sin,
   use temp'rance and discipline.
   Have mercy, Lord!

8. Steal not; all usury abhor
   nor wring their life-blood from the poor,
   but open wide thy loving hand
   to all the poor in the land.
   Have mercy, Lord!

9. Bear not false witness nor belie
   thy neighbor by false calumny.
   Defend his innocence from blame;
   with charity hide his shame.
   Have mercy, Lord!

10. Thy neighbor's house desire thou not,
    his wife, nor aught that he hath got,
    but wish that his such good may be
    as thy heart doth wish for thee.
    Have mercy, Lord!

11. God these commandments gave therein
    to show thee, child of man, thy sin
    and make thee also well perceive
    how man unto God should live.
    Have mercy, Lord!

12. Help us, Lord Jesus Christ, for we
    a mediator have in thee;
    our works cannot salvation gain;
    they merit but endless pain.
    Have mercy, Lord!

Text: Exodus 20:1-17, vers. Martin Luther, 1524; tr. Richard Massie, 1854, alt. Tune: DIES SIND DIE HEILGEN, German melody, c. 1200.

To Jordan Came the Christ, Our Lord

1. To Jordan came the Christ, our Lord,
to do his Father's pleasure;
baptized by John, the Father's Word
was given us to treasure.
This heav'nly washing now shall be
a cleansing from transgression
and, by his blood and agony,
release from death's oppression.
A new life now awaits us.

2. Oh, hear and mark the message well,
for God himself has spoken.
Let faith, not doubt, among us dwell
and so receive this token.
Our Lord here with his Word endows
pure water, freely flowing.
God's Holy Spirit here avows
our kinship, while bestowing
the baptism of his blessing.

3. These truths on Jordan's banks were
    shown
by mighty word and wonder.
The Father's voice from heav'n came
    down,
which we do well to ponder:
"This man is my beloved Son,
in whom my heart has pleasure.
Him you must hear, and him alone,
and trust in fullest measure
the word that he has spoken."

4. There stood the Son of God in love,
his grace to us extending;
the Holy Spirit like a dove
upon the scene descending;
the triune God assuring us,
with promises compelling,
that in our baptism he will thus
among us find a dwelling
to comfort and sustain us.

5. To his disciples spoke the Lord,
"Go out to ev'ry nation,
and bring to them the living Word
and this my invitation:
Let ev'ryone abandon sin
and come in true contrition
to be baptized, and thereby win
full pardon and remission,
and heav'nly bliss inherit."

6. But woe to those who cast aside
this grace so freely given;
they shall in sin and shame abide
and to despair be driven.
For born in sin, their works must fail,
their striving saves them never;
their pious acts do not avail,
and they are lost forever,
eternal death their portion.

7. All that the mortal eye beholds
is water as we pour it.
Before the eye of faith unfolds
the pow'r of Jesus' merit.
For here it sees the crimson flood
to all our ills bring healing;
the wonders of his precious blood
the love of God revealing,
assuring his own pardon.

Text: Martin Luther; tr. Elizabeth Quitmeyer, 1911–88, alt. Tune: CHRIST, UNSER HERR, J. Walter, *Geistliche Gesangbüchlein*, 1524.

MOVIES ABOUT MARTIN LUTHER—AN OVERVIEW

Despite having lived five hundred years ago, Martin Luther remains one of the most influential people in the history of Western civilization. And parts of his life story are quite dramatic. It's no surprise, then, that filmmakers have periodically attempted to make movies about Luther. What may be surprising is that these films take quite divergent tacks on the storytelling. Each has strengths, but for different audiences and purposes. Presented here are brief synopses and reviews of four films about the life of Martin Luther—three of them available on Netflix (as of this writing), and the fourth available online.

Martin Luther (1953)
Directed by Irving Pichel
Luther played by Niall MacGinnis
Available through Netflix (DVD.com)

This movie is over sixty years old, and the film quality shows it: it would benefit greatly from a digital remastering. It is in black and white, with a soundtrack typical of the 1950s. In many ways, though, it has held up surprisingly well. MacGinnis plays Luther in a pleasantly understated manner, with good support from John Ruddock as Johann von Staupitz. Philipp Melanchthon, Luther's right-hand man, played by Guy Verney, has an appropriately large supporting role too. This film gets most of the historical detail correct, no doubt helped in that regard by consultants such as Jaroslav Pelikan and Theodore Tappert. For instance, there are no pews in the churches, and the settings like the Diet of Worms look plausible. Yes, Luther does nail the Ninety-Five Theses to the church door, but he also speaks of mailing a copy to the archbishop (which was, historically, the primary "posting"). The dramatic high point is the Diet before the emperor, but the Augsburg Confession gets its due. Overall, this is a pretty reliable general-purpose video introduction to the Lutheran Reformation.

Luther (1973)
Directed by Guy Green
Luther played by Stacy Keach
Available through Netflix (DVD.com)

Here we have basically a filming of John Osborne's 1961 stage play by the same name. It is a much headier, interior depiction than in the other movies. Building on the psychological understanding of Luther and his actions that was becoming prevalent at the time, we see a tormented monk and priest. While this certainly was an important aspect of the reformer as he wrestled with his uncertainties about pleasing God, other aspects are missing that would make it more suitable as an overview to the Reformation. One of the film's focuses is on an episode that is largely absent from the other films, the Peasants' Revolt. Luther's writings were seen by some as a call to overthrow rulers, a move which Luther disavowed. In fact, he counseled the rulers to bar no holds in putting down the revolt. The result was a bloodbath for which some, including a character in this movie, blame the reformer. Film buffs will enjoy notable cast members such as Judi Dench as Katharina von Bora and Maurice Denham as Johann von Staupitz.

Martin Luther: Heretic (1983)
Directed by Norman Stone
Luther played by Jonathan Pryce
Not available as of this writing

This made-for-television movie was produced by the British Broadcasting Corporation (BBC) in commemoration of the 500th anniversary of Martin Luther's birth in 1483. It is unfortunate that it isn't currently available (though perhaps it will be rereleased), because it is a compelling depiction of the core of Luther's ministry. True, Jonathan Pryce comes across as lean and intense throughout, and we miss Luther's famous earthiness, but that is a common failing in these films. But most of the main characters (Luther, Staupitz, Frederick, Eck, Spalatin, Karlstadt, Charles) are portrayed clearly, as are the primary events in Luther's early career.

Luther (2003)
Directed by Eric Till
Luther played by Joseph Fiennes
Available through Netflix (DVD.com)

The most recent of the major Luther movies, this is also in many ways the most watchable and the most holistic in terms of treating Luther's life. It does deal with his anxiety over finding a loving God, as any life of Luther must, but also shows that indulgences were present long before Tetzel, presents Katharina von Bora as a strong character, and extends to the important presentation of the Augsburg Confession in 1530. There are a few anachronisms, most obviously Luther preaching while (a) roaming among a congregation (b) seated by families (c) in pews—three of them right there!—but they are only minor flaws in an excellent presentation. The sets are impressive: Wittenberg is seen with the original tower on the Castle Church, and the Wartburg Castle, too, is seen minus the large tower that was a later addition. Plus, the general messiness of life in late medieval times is on full display. For overall help in understanding Luther's life and times, this is probably the best of the lot.

Also worthy of mention is the two-part PBS presentation *Martin Luther* (2002), available for viewing online. Not a complete dramatization of his life, it does present important scenes, interspersed with commentaries by various scholars.

Finally, a new movie and a new television program are in production as this Sourcebook is being assembled, both of them with the participation of the ELCA.

Martin Luther

To be broadcast on PBS in 2017.

A new documentary filmed in Europe with a large cast and crew. Luther scholar Dr. Erik Herrmann was on location in Poland to ensure accuracy. Sponsored by Thrivent Financial.

Rick Steves's Luther and the Reformation

To be broadcast on PBS in 2017.

A trip through the sites of Luther's life and Reformation, guided by ELCA member Rick Steves.

A CONTEMPORARY LUTHERAN APPROACH TO INTERRELIGIOUS RELATIONS
Why Follow Luther Past 2017?

ELCA Consultative Panel on Lutheran–Jewish Relations

The 500th anniversary of the Reformation provides an opportunity to reflect on Martin Luther's legacy. Does it help or hinder peaceful relations with individuals in other religions?

On first impression, the legacy seems unhelpful. Martin Luther lived in late medieval Christendom (a religiously based and religiously unified society in which only Christians could be citizens). Interreligious relations were never his central concern. To be sure, he could acknowledge the way God provided good gifts (of parental love, food, and shelter, for example) to Muslim children as well as to Christian children. He opposed a crusade against Muslims. Early in his career, he urged Christians to treat Jews with respect. But anti-Judaism sentiment surfaced frequently in his lectures, and his harsh treatises of the 1540s called on rulers to destroy synagogues, burn books, and deny safe passage to Jews. In these respects, his own advice and behavior do not provide a model for Christians today. For this reason his harshly anti-Jewish statements have been repudiated by a variety of Lutheran churches. [The 1994 ELCA statement "Declaration of the ELCA to the Jewish Community" is at www.ELCA.org/en/Resources/Ecumenical-and-Inter-Religious-Relations.]

However, Luther's statements against the Jews in the 1540s violated some of his own principles [see Eric Gritsch, cited below]. To choose but one example, Luther regarded God to be both hidden and revealed. Even with faith and the aid of the scriptures, even with God's self-disclosure in Jesus the Christ, humans cannot fully understand God or God's actions. According to the book of Romans, one item hidden from view is God's future judgment about the Jews. Paul ends his discussion of this topic with a doxology of praise (Rom. 11:33-36), acknowledging the mystery of God. Luther's claim in the 1540s to know God's hidden judgments (about the Jews) therefore not only failed to heed Paul, it also violated his own limits regarding what can be known.

Far more helpful are the underlying principles of Luther's theology. They open exciting and fruitful possibilities for a more respectful and workable understanding of interreligious relations. They can equip Christians to engage Jews and others in positive, constructive, and honest ways. We propose for consideration four of his signature principles.

1. A very basic principle for Luther is that God adopts people solely out of God's generosity, without any prerequisites. Humans are in no position to control or limit this generosity. Faith, for Luther, is primarily a matter of trust—trusting God's promises. The benefit of faith is not that it makes a person eligible for grace; the value of faith is that it celebrates and receives the benefits of God's generosity. Faith acknowledges what God has done, is already doing, and will do. What too often happens, however, is that "justification by grace through faith" gets understood to mean that a human must first have faith in Jesus, and then God will do the saving. This view ("you must first have faith") then produces a boundary that separates Christians from non-Christians in a way that limits God's generosity. To say that we do not know the limits of God's generosity is also to say that we do not know how far the good effects of God's generosity extend. In other words, with regard both to other Christians and to non-Christians, the mysteries of God's judgment and salvation ultimately remain beyond our knowing.

Luther was clear that no one could know for certain another person's relationship with God. The calling of the Christian is to share the good news of God's grace, not to decide who needs it and who does not. God's generosity is paramount, and the good news of that remarkable generosity is a principle we can claim and proclaim loudly and with joy.

2. Luther asserted that God is active in the world in such a way as to empower but not to control. Nothing can exist without God's sustaining power. Creation is ongoing. God is active in every realm of life, working in and through nature and other human beings, through social structures and individual actions, to bring good gifts to humans. The gospel enables us to see the consistency between the way God treats the chosen people (Israel and the church) and the way God treats the world as a whole. Every human is gifted by God. No one, in whatever religion, is beyond the pale of God's gifting. (Whether any specific person recognizes and acknowledges God as the source of her or his gifts is another question.)

God values all creation—across all differences. This principle can be reflected in our behavior and our attitude toward individuals in other religions.

3. A third principle to which Luther clung is a theology of the cross. This was Luther's alternative to scholasticism. The medieval scholastics endeavored to answer questions that the Bible did not. They began with a biblical or doctrinal idea and then used logical inference to fill in the gap. As the distinction (between what was revealed and what was inferred) faded from view, every part of scholastic teaching seemed equally authorized by revelation. People were tempted to believe they could have the whole truth in one package. Luther objected. He emphasized the limits of our knowing. God has disclosed enough for us to know God's gracious disposition toward us and to know something of God's character and purpose, but this knowing does not answer our every question or provide us with the whole truth. If our knowing were complete, there would be no point in dialogue. Because our knowing is limited, dialogue—interreligious and otherwise—is valuable.

Moreover, Luther emphasized the experiential and/or relational dimension of our knowing. We know God from within a relationship with God (whether healthy or broken) and not from some neutral stance. Our understanding of God can deepen with experience. A crucial dimension of this experiential knowing is suffering. God is seen more clearly through suffering (including the suffering of Jesus, the suffering of others, and one's own suffering) than through success. Humans are connected to each other through the commonality and universality of human suffering. And the purpose of the promises made by the God most fully revealed in the cross and resurrection is not to insulate humans from suffering but to "be with" them and to call them to "be with" others. A theology of the cross excludes triumphalism; we who know God's promise of gracious, trustworthy love need not have all the answers as we acknowledge the deep mysteries of God. We can live humbly within these limits and still stand in courageous solidarity and loving compassion with *all* who suffer.

4. Another central principle is Luther's high regard for vocation as a calling from God. The person who benefits from God's generosity is called to serve the neighbor and the community. To serve is to listen attentively. To serve is to care actively about the whole person and about the quality of relationships in the community as a whole. To serve is to exercise the radical freedom that accompanies grace. It is to be informed by the scriptures but not enslaved to any detailed codes of conduct, such as those sometimes drawn up by various Christian authors. As Jews and Christians alike recognize, the scriptures teach that God's goal is shalom (peace/ wholeness/ justice). We who enjoy God's generosity are called to participate in God's project of fostering this shalom. This principle of service to the neighbor can undergird all interreligious cooperation.

When these four key principles are taken together, the basis for interreligious relations is a humble need to connect with others and to engage in dialogue. Christians simply do not know enough to be able to claim that they have God figured out—or even to have humans figured out, for that matter. In interreligious dialogue, just as Christians draw on their own deep and rich tradition for crucial insights to offer others, so they benefit from many of the insights offered by their dialogue partners.

Of particular urgency is dialogue with our Jewish neighbors, because no other religion has as much in common with Christianity as does Judaism. We read the same sacred texts (though ordered differently, the Jewish Bible contains the same books as the Protestant Old Testament), we worship the same God, we celebrate God's steadfast love, and together we are called to foster shalom and to mend the world. While recognizing significant differences, Jews and Christians can find mutually beneficial ways to work together, learn from each other, and support each other in the face of adversity, misunderstanding, or hostility. Jews have an ongoing covenantal calling to be a blessing to the world. Christians have a special responsibility to overcome the tragic, centuries-old legacy of anti-Judaism and anti-Semitism, while at the same time opposing the misrepresentation and mistreatment of any other religious group.

The common experience of individuals who have engaged in interreligious dialogue is that their understanding and appreciation of their own tradition is enhanced in the process. Sometimes this comes about smoothly; at other times it comes from wrestling with deep and troubling challenges. Dialogue invites everyone to go deeper. The goal is not to discover uniformity. Participants instead begin to sense the permeability of human boundaries, the possibility of shalom, and the underlying commonality of the human condition. They discover a deeper sense of their own vocation.

In this way Luther's principles undergird an outlook that differs markedly from some of his own conclusions. This outlook enables his followers to come to terms with religious pluralism five hundred years later. It allows us to be faithful even as we embrace and give thanks for new possibilities.

Resources

Gritsch, Eric. *Martin Luther's Anti-Semitism: Against His Better Judgment.* Grand Rapids: Eerdmans, 2012.

Jodock, Darrell, ed. *Covenantal Conversations: Christians in Dialogue with Jews and Judaism.* Minneapolis: Fortress Press, 2008.

Schramm, Brooks, and Kirsi Stjerna, eds. *Martin Luther, the Bible, and the Jewish People: A Reader.* Minneapolis: Fortress Press, 2012.

The Consultative Panel on Lutheran–Jewish Relations is a small group of ELCA pastors and professors appointed by the presiding bishop. Its role is to assist the various expressions of the ELCA to increase cooperation and understanding between Lutheran Christians and the Jewish community. It does this by working with the staff of Ecumenical and Inter-Religious Relations to offer advice, develop educational materials, and maintain contact with Jewish leaders. The members of the Consultative Panel, as of January 2014, were Darrell Jodock (chair), Ward "Skip" Cornett III, Esther Menn, Peter Pettit, and Margaret "Peg" Schultz-Akerson. Kathryn Lohre, Ecumenical and Inter-Religious Relations staff. Thank you to Michael Chan for his assistance in the preparation of this document.

THE LUTHERAN REFORMATION IN CONTEXT

Reformation	Rest of world

1400

Jan Hus burned at the stake 1415

Chinese capital moved from Nanking (Nanjing) to Peking (Beijing) 1420

1425

Joan of Arc burned at the stake 1431

Inca Dynasty founded 1438

1450 Printing press invented by Johannes Gutenberg 1450

Machu Picchu constructed c. 1450

Constantinople falls to Ottoman army, becomes Istanbul 1453

1475

Spanish Inquisition begins 1481

Luther born 1483

Morocco invades Mali 1488

Christopher Columbus lands in the Americas 1492

Katharina von Bora born 1499

1500

Michelangelo begins work on the statue David 1501

Atlantic slave trade begins 1502

Leonardo da Vinci begins painting the Mona Lisa 1503

Luther becomes a monk 1505

Smallpox hits the New World in Hispaniola 1507

Luther called to Wittenberg faculty 1512

Copernicus declares the sun is at the center of the solar system 1512

Luther posts the Ninety-Five Theses 1517

Melanchthon joins Wittenberg faculty 1518

Leipzig Disputation 1519

Spanish conquest of Mexico 1519

Luther excommunicated 1521

Luther appears at the Diet (Assembly) of Worms 1521

Luther declared an outlaw, escorted to the Wartburg Castle 1521

Magellan and Elcano complete first circumnavigation of the earth 1522

Luther translates New Testament into German 1522

Sweden becomes independent 1523

Chocolate comes to Europe 1523

Peasants' War in Germany 1524

1525   Luther marries Katharina von Bora 1525

Lutheran Reformation in Sweden begins 1527

Luther writes "A Mighty Fortress" c. 1528

Luther publishes his Small Catechism 1529

Augsburg Confession signed 1530

Church of England breaks away from Roman Catholic Church 1531

Luther (with others) translates Old Testament into German 1534

Cartier claims Quebec for France 1534

William Tyndale's partial translation of the Bible into English published 1537

Luther publishes On the Jews and Their Lies 1543

Council of Trent begins meeting 1545

Luther dies 1546

Michelangelo becomes chief architect of St. Peter's Basilica, Rome 1546

Francis Xavier works in Indonesia 1546

Henry VIII dies 1547

1550

ABOUT THE LUTHERANS

BULLETIN INSERTS

As part of this resource, twelve bulletin inserts have been prepared, dealing with diverse aspects of the Lutheran church, historically and today. The bulletin inserts on pages 133–156 of this Sourcebook are also available as full color PDF files on the CD-ROM bound with this book. Unaltered inserts may be reproduced and distributed in print or electronically by the purchaser of this volume for onetime, non-sale use, provided copies are for local use only and the printed copyright notice appears.

There is no recommended schedule for use of these bulletin inserts—that is left up to the user's discretion. If there are additional topics that you wish were covered, we encourage you to create your own, similar inserts. If you would like to share them with a wider audience, that can be done by offering them on the ELCA's Reformation website, elca500.org.

The bulletin inserts are reproduced for your convenience on the following pages.

ABOUT THE LUTHERANS
Martin Luther: Monk to Reformer

We live in an era when fame is highly desired. Whether it's getting hits on social media, getting invited to desirable gatherings, or making it big in Hollywood or Nashville, people want to be known, to be memorable—often for the wrong reasons. It's noteworthy, then, that in 2017 the Lutheran church—and the world—marks a big anniversary involving one of our own (our founder, actually). Martin Luther didn't intend to become famous, and yet he changed the world, helping to usher in the modern era.

This little sheet doesn't have room to detail Luther's life and accomplishments, and you will probably be hearing a lot about them from many sources, so this will just provide a brief overview.

Martin Luther was born in 1483 in what is now central Germany but then was a separate principality called Saxony. His parents tried to give him a good education and hoped he would become a lawyer. Instead, when he was twenty-one he became a Catholic monk. He wanted to earn God's love but was tormented by the sense that he could never be good enough. He punished himself mercilessly until finally a wise mentor sent him to study and teach Bible at the then new University of Wittenberg.

Wittenberg in 1536

Not long after he arrived there, he became incensed by the church saying, in effect, that if people bought a certain document—an indulgence—it would provide God's forgiveness for their (or a loved one's) sins. Being a

REFORMATION 500

Martin Luther

university professor, he wrote a list of ninety-five sentences to debate about the topic. That list, the Ninety-Five Theses, stirred up a hornet's nest in the church and began the Reformation. He made them public on October 31, 1517—coming up on five hundred years ago.

For challenging the church and refusing to back down, Luther was called before the Holy Roman emperor, Charles V, at a meeting in the imperial city of Worms. Asked to take back what he had written, he refused and was declared an outlaw. Anyone could have captured him and killed him or turned him in to authorities, in which case his death was likely. Fortunately, his own prince protected him, hiding him out in a castle where he began translating the Bible into German. In the process, he helped create the standard German language.

Luther wrote many influential books, most of which are still valued today. He created the Small Catechism to guide ordinary people in learning about God. He wrote hymns such as "A mighty fortress is our God." He was a passionate, sometimes crudely mannered man, and in later life he wrote terrible, cruel things about the Jewish people, statements for which the Lutheran church has apologized.

Yet Luther was a remarkable man, helping to create the modern notion of what it means to be an individual, not just an atom in a sea of molecules, and, of course, reviving and reforming the church. He is a man worth celebrating!

ABOUT THE LUTHERANS

Martin Luther's German Bible

What version of the Bible do you hear and read? Just in English, we have many to choose from. They range from translations that aim to be as accurate as possible (such as the New Revised Standard Version) to others whose main objective is to be easy to understand, even if certain details get lost.

Imagine, though, if there were no Bible available in English—if such a thing didn't exist. What if the only Bible was in a language most didn't know and we had to rely on priests and scholars to tell us what was in the Bible? That was the situation in the Germany of Martin Luther's time. The Bible was most commonly found in Latin, though scholars could read it in the original languages of Hebrew and Greek. An important part of Luther's reforms was recognizing that a German Bible was needed—and then actually creating it!

Sometimes things happen because it's the right time, and that seems to be the case with Luther's Bible. Johannes Gutenberg's invention of printing with movable type had come along a few decades earlier and was coming into widespread use. Luther recognized the need to provide a Bible that ordinary, literate people could read. The many dialects of the German people were beginning to coalesce into a form that was widely understandable. Luther even had an artist friend, Lucas Cranach, who could provide illustrations for the Bible, aiding people's

The Wartburg Castle as it would have appeared in Luther's time

Title page from an early printing of Luther's translation

understanding. And finally, Luther had the time to devote to the project.

The dispute with the Roman Catholic hierarchy that had begun with indulgences and Luther's Ninety-Five Theses had expanded and now came to a head with the imperial council (or "diet") held at Worms. Luther strongly defended his writings but still was condemned as an outlaw (in addition to already being named a heretic). He could have been arrested and executed, but his prince, Frederick the Wise, "kidnapped" him in April 1521 and hid him away in the Wartburg Castle. There the reformer had little to do, so he set out to begin his translation of the Bible.

He started with the New Testament. He had learned New Testament (*koine*) Greek, the original language, and so began with that, not Latin. Since the German language was still evolving, Luther would make trips into nearby towns to hear how people actually spoke. Luther returned to his home in Wittenberg in 1522, and within six months, his New Testament was published. After that he worked with other pastors and scholars to prepare the Old Testament. The complete Bible, with 117 woodcut illustrations, was first published in 1534. He revised it several times up until his death.

Luther's work on a German Bible was a landmark achievement. It influenced others in many countries, including England, to do the same. He brought the scriptures into the language of his people, and in so doing spread the gospel.

ABOUT THE LUTHERANS
Luther's Small Catechism

Of all the things Martin Luther wrote, he is probably best known for two things: the hymn "A mighty fortress is our God" and the Small Catechism. Interestingly, Luther himself was ambivalent about the lasting value of most of his writings, with two exceptions—and one of them was this little pamphlet, the Small Catechism. And this from someone whose writings changed the whole landscape of the Western religious world.

Most of us know the Small Catechism well. Many spent hours memorizing it as teens. But how did it come to be, and what is it that makes it so helpful?

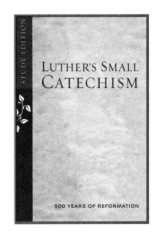

In 2017 we are observing the 500th anniversary of the Reformation's start, when Luther posted the Ninety-Five Theses. If that was the act of a passionate young man, a decade later he was facing the needs of the church he was reforming. If it was no longer enough just to go through the motions, following the lead of a Latin-rite priest, then what was at the heart of what people needed to know—and how were they to learn that? To meet that need, Luther the pastor and teacher created two catechisms—the Large (primarily intended for pastors) and the Small (for use in the home).

A catechism is a document that lays out the basic ideas of religion in a simple question-and-answer format. For the Small Catechism, Luther chose to open up some of the basics of Christian faith: the Ten Commandments, the Apostles' Creed, the Lord's Prayer, the sacraments of Holy Baptism

REFORMATION 500

and Holy Communion, and the Office of the Keys and Confession. It's worth noticing that he based this teaching document on what already existed rather than starting from scratch and inventing a whole new system. Luther was committed to the church catholic.

From a 1550 edition

His genius is shown in the way he opened up these statements of faith. The famous question in each case was, in German, "*Was ist das*?" In English, most of us know this as "What does this mean?" but a literal translation would be "What is *that?*" And then he proceeded to tell, in beautifully simple language, what each commandment, each part of the creed, each petition of the Lord's Prayer, tells us about God and about us as God's children. These explanations set out a God who is not the stern judge of Luther's own childhood, but a loving parent who offers us unconditional grace and only then invites us to live accordingly.

How profound was Luther's achievement in writing the Small Catechism? A mark of it can be seen in the simple fact that nearly five hundred years after its first publication in 1529, and after being translated into hundreds of languages, it is still one of the most effective tools for learning and teaching what the Christian faith is all about.

ABOUT THE LUTHERANS
The Augsburg Confession

The Augsburg Confession, written in the midst of the Reformation tumult, is the core statement of what Lutherans believe. It was produced in 1530, thirteen years after young professor Martin Luther posted the Ninety-Five Theses in Wittenberg. A lot had happened in those thirteen years. Thanks to Luther's creative exploration of the gospel and its implications, his colorful personality (opponents had other adjectives), and the availability of the printing press, his views on religious matters as well as the politics of the day had been widely distributed. In many parts of central Europe, people were responding favorably, to the consternation of the Church of Rome, which had been accustomed to being the single expression of the Christian church in that region.

In the sixteenth century there was no nation called Germany. Rather, the various duchies and electorates made up a key part of the Holy Roman Empire, a remnant of the European territory once governed by ancient Rome. For much of Reformation times, Charles V governed as Holy

Presentation of Augsburg Confession

Roman Emperor. He had watched his empire become increasingly fractured by divisions among princes favorable to Luther and other reformers, and those who kept their loyalty to Rome and the pope. The emperor needed the princes to be unified, not least because a Turkish invasion of Europe had reached the gates of Vienna. And so, in January 1530, the emperor called for a diet, or general assembly, in the German city of Augsburg. He asked the German princes and imperial cities to explain their religious convictions.

REFORMATION 500

And so, reforming theologians and the rulers who supported them headed for Augsburg—among them, Luther's colleague Philipp Melanchthon and his pastor, Johannes Bugenhagen. Luther himself could not accompany them because he had been named an outlaw at a previous diet. He had also been excommunicated by the pope. He was, however, consulted on the final text via mail.

Philipp Melanchthon

Upon their arrival in Augsburg, Melanchthon, consulting with previous preliminary documents, composed the final text of the confession. The German princes who favored the Reformation viewpoint agreed to it and signed it. On June 25, 1530, the Augsburg Confession was read aloud in German before the emperor and presented in written form in both German and Latin.

The Augsburg Confession (sometimes called Augustana from its Latin title) is now found in a larger collection of Lutheran confessional writings called *The Book of Concord*. It contains twenty-eight parts, or articles. The first twenty-one of these stress points of agreement with the Roman Church of the time, though sometimes with crucial differences. In the last seven, the writers lay out what they see as abuses committed by the church.

The Augsburg Confession continues to guide the teachings of Lutheran churches to this day. Though a product of troubled times, it is filled with witness to the gospel of Jesus Christ.

ABOUT THE LUTHERANS

Women and the Reformation

Argula von Grumbach

"I am prepared to lose everything, even life or limb. May God stand by me." So wrote Argula von Grumbach (1492–1563/68?) from Bavaria, who found Martin Luther's message of Christian freedom and equality empowering. This noble woman challenged an entire Catholic university in Ingolstadt in defense of Lutheran faith and a student persecuted for "Lutheran heresy." This best-selling lay author with her letter-treatises eventually disappeared under pressure from male authorities. Luther considered her a valiant hero of faith.

The Protestant principles "scripture alone," "grace alone," and "priesthood of all believers" inspired women just like men to reengage Christian faith and find renewed spiritual meaning in their daily vocations. With the newly written catechisms and hymns, women were equipped to teach the revived faith to their households, where they exercised significant leadership in matters of religious practice. Women lost the monastic option as convents were closed in Protestant areas, but they benefited significantly from the education provided even for peasant girls.

Whereas the Reformation theology proclaimed equality in Christian love and freedom from human-made bonds, women were forbidden to preach or teach in public. Motherhood was presented to women as the holiest of callings, on a par with that of apostles and bishops. So women used creativity in embracing their domestic calling and the authority it brought along.

REFORMATION 500

Katharine Schütz Zell (1498–1562), a widely published lay author who had no children of her own, identified herself with a calling of a "church mother." In this role she exercised pastoral authority by the side of her pastor-husband in Strasbourg, even daring to preach at funerals. Her scintillating writings in defense of marriage may have caused an uproar, yet her pastoral texts and a hymnbook demonstrate her desire to promote ecumenical unity and to empower Christians to sing the gospel with new voices. Like von Grumbach, she also corresponded with Luther.

Another associate of Luther was Duchess Elisabeth von Braunschweig (1485–1555), who used her authority as the "mother of the people in her land" to implement Lutheran faith through legislation. Like her own mother earlier, Elisabeth had suffered exile from her Catholic husband and children once she confessed her faith in public by receiving the sacrament in a Lutheran rite. Her advice to her son, whom she groomed as a Lutheran ruler, was that he should obey God, the emperor—and his mother.

Of all the Reformation mothers, the most famous is Luther's beloved Katharina von Bora (1499–1552). She won the heart and admiration of Luther, who had orchestrated the escape of Katharina and eleven other nuns from their convent. As his equal "partner in calamity," Katharina mothered their six children and managed the intricate finances and other affairs of their bustling household. Luther admitted that next to the Holy Spirit, he obeyed his wife-"lord," Katharina.

Katharina von Bora

These and other mothers of faith took significant risks and endured criticism if not even persecution for their choices. Their involvement was crucial for the new faith to take root.

Kirsi Stjerna

ABOUT THE LUTHERANS

The Reformation Spreads in Europe

Martin Luther is, deservedly, receiving most of the attention as we mark the beginning of the Reformation in Saxony. But with remarkable speed, those teachings spread to other countries in Europe. How did that occur? Largely through the work of some courageous leaders. Let's look at how the Reformation came to a few countries whose descendants have helped shape the ELCA.

Statue of Olaus and Laurentius Petri

In **Sweden**, two brothers, Olavus and Laurentius Petri, spearheaded the Reformation. Both had studied theology with Luther in Wittenberg. They returned to Sweden around the same time King Gustav I Vasa was creating an independent nation. He made Olavus pastor of the city church in Stockholm, where he translated the New Testament into Swedish, created a catechism, published an order of worship, and provided a Swedish hymnal. Meanwhile his younger brother, Laurentius, was made the first Lutheran archbishop of Sweden; he and Olavus jointly produced a complete Bible in Swedish.

In **Denmark**, too, the Reformation came early. As in Sweden, it was led by a young man who had studied under Luther in Wittenberg—Hans Tausen. The ruler at the time, Frederick I, was formally opposed to Reformation ideas, but he protected Tausen and tolerated Lutheran writings. The next king, Christian III, stripped the Roman Catholic Church of its wealth, and Luther's pastor, Johannes Bugenhagen, made a journey from Wittenberg to crown the king and help organize the Danish church.

REFORMATION 500

Norway was, at the time, ruled by Denmark, and initially the spread of the Reformation there was slower. Christian III tried to encourage its growth there, but at first there wasn't much popular support; it was more of a top-down reformation. Nevertheless, pastors such as Jorgen Eriksson, who would become bishop of Stavanger, preached Lutheran teachings, and the Reformation gradually took hold.

Mikael Agricola was yet another student of Luther, and it was he who led the Reformation in **Finland**. At that time, Finland was ruled by Sweden. The first Lutheran bishop of Turku (and thus of Finland), Martinus Skytte, left most Roman Catholic orders in place. Agricola's ministry as the next bishop, though, mirrored much of Luther's: he translated the New Testament into Finnish, and in the process created the Finnish literary language. He prepared

Mikael Agricola

a prayer book in Finnish, created a vernacular order of communion, and collected Finnish hymns. He was also the first married bishop of Turku.

Moving southeast from Wittenberg, **Slovakia** is another area where the Reformation took hold. Two visionary people must receive much of the credit. Jan Hus lived about a century before Luther and ministered in neighboring Bohemia (now the Czech Republic), but his reforming teachings influenced Slovak Christians, as they did Martin Luther himself. So the way was prepared for the Reformation from Wittenberg. And in the early seventeenth century, another graduate of the University of Wittenberg, Jiří (or Juraj) Třanovský, helped cement the Reformation in Slovakia by translating many hymns and collecting them into a hymnal called *Cithara Sanctorum* ("Lyre of the Saints").

Lutherans from these lands and many others came to America, establishing first separate enclaves, but gradually merging with other Lutherans into church bodies, including our current Evangelical Lutheran Church in America.

ABOUT THE LUTHERANS

Lutherans Come to North America

Most of us know that Lutheranism had its start in Germany with Martin Luther. But when and how did it come over to North America? The story begins with the arrival of a pastor with a distinctive name, at least to our ears. On April 17, 1640, Swedish pastor Reorus Torkillus arrived in Fort Christina, near present-day Wilmington, Delaware. The Swedish government was developing a small settlement there and needed someone to attend to the spiritual needs of the Swedish immigrants.

If we wish to see a sustained presence of Lutherans, though, we must wait about a hundred years. Germans had begun arriving in America in the 1680s, with most settling in Pennsylvania and upstate New York but others heading for Louisiana and the southeastern colonies. Many were fleeing poor conditions in Germany, and though they brought their beliefs from home, there was, at first, no provision for Lutheran pastors. But in 1741 Lutherans in Pennsylvania issued a call to a thirty-year-old pastor in Saxony, Henry Melchior Muhlenberg. He arrived in Philadelphia in 1742. Muhlenberg turned out to be an excellent choice. Not only was he untiring in his pastoral work, but he laid the foundations for what would become the Lutheran church in America. He helped more congregations to organize and call pastors. He called into existence the first North American organization of Lutherans, the Ministerium of Pennsylvania. He helped prepare a standard Lutheran liturgy and create a constitution. He even contributed deeply to a hymnal published in 1786.

Henry Melchior Muhlenberg

REFORMATION 500

Lutherans kept coming from different European lands. Swedes and Norwegians settled largely in the upper Midwest; Danes were more widespread. German immigrants were concentrated in a band across the northern part of the country, but they also established concentrations in places like Missouri and Texas. Slovaks, heirs to Luther's predecessor Jan Hus, also arrived. Often these groups set up their own separate church systems, such as the Augustana Synod, the Norwegian Synod, and the German-based General Synod. Then there were groups that formed in opposition to teachings of the earlier groups, like the Hauge Synod and the Missouri Synod. Mergers have occurred, but so have divisions. Currently the Evangelical Lutheran Church in America is by far the largest Lutheran body in the United States, followed by the Lutheran Church–Missouri Synod and many smaller bodies.

But the story doesn't end with the first immigrations from northern Europe. The nineteenth century brought increased missionary activity to the scene, and in time some of those who had been  taught by these missionaries also came to North America, bringing their own Lutheran customs. So now our mix includes heritages such as Ethiopian, Nigerian, Liberian, Korean, Chinese, Indian, Palestinian, Brazilian, and many more. Where can your congregation trace its roots?

ABOUT THE LUTHERANS
Lutherans in the Caribbean

Lutheran churches have deep roots in northern Europe and have large numbers in North America. Partner churches are flourishing in the Middle East, southern Africa, Australia, and Asia. But many Lutherans don't know that there have been Lutherans in some parts of the Caribbean for almost four hundred years.

Historically, Lutheranism came to the Caribbean as the religion of white European and, later, American settlers. But in time some of these churches opened their doors to local inhabitants, Hispanics, African Americans, and Native Americans. Some of these congregations have become truly indigenous and multicultural ministries. More recently, North Americans moved and settled in some parts of the Caribbean, beginning other congregations for expatriates and vacationers.

Frederick Lutheran Church, Charlotte Amalie

The oldest Lutheran congregation in the Caribbean was founded in the Virgin Islands in 1666 by Danish settlers on the island of St. Thomas, the Frederick congregation in Charlotte Amalie. They later founded other congregations on the islands of St. Croix, St. John, and St. Thomas in the eighteenth century. Although these congregations were originally intended for Danes, by the 1750s they were ministering to the enslaved Africans on the islands.

When Denmark sold these islands to the United States in 1917, these congregations affiliated with American Lutheran denominations. There are also several congregations of Virgin Island Lutherans on the mainland of the United States, most notably in New York City.

REFORMATION 500

Similarly, Dutch Lutherans founded congregations in the area of Guyana and Suriname in the eighteenth century, as the Europeans planted colonies there. Congregations generally consisted of white settlers and their descendants until the middle of the nineteenth century, when they began to reach out to other populations. Guyana is especially racially diverse, and the Lutheran congregations there include African Americans, Native Americans, East Indians, and some Chinese.

Though it has a long history of European colonization, Lutherans did not become established on Puerto Rico until it became a part of the United States in 1898. In that year a young student, Gustav Swenson, moved to Puerto Rico and eventually started a Lutheran congregation there. He was eventually followed by a number of different pastors and missionaries from the United States, who began to preach in Spanish to the local population.

Lutheran congregations can be found in some of the other islands of the Caribbean. There is a small Lutheran presence in Cuba. Antigua, Bermuda, and the Bahamas all have Lutheran congregations affiliated with various bodies. Even Haiti hosts a Lutheran enclave, connected with the Church of the Lutheran Confession in Alsace and Lorraine (France).

Although many of these Caribbean Lutheran congregations were begun by Europeans or Americans, either as settlers or missionaries, most of their members are now predominantly local people—Virgin Islanders, Guyanese and Surinamese, Puerto Ricans, and others. They may be Hispanic, Native American, African American, or other local populations, worshiping in Spanish, English, French, or other local languages. These congregations enrich the palate of world Lutheranism, and help spread the gospel of Christ into every corner of the world.

Mark Granquist

ABOUT THE LUTHERANS

Lutherans around the World

Wittenberg was a small provincial town on the edge of the empire when professor and pastor Martin Luther lit an evangelical spark that illuminated God's grace and prompted reform in the Western church. Over the next five hundred years the good news spread far beyond Saxony and Europe. Today the family of Lutheran churches includes both the Lutheran World Federation (with 72 million congregants in 145 church bodies in ninety-eight nations) and the International Lutheran Council (with thirty-five member bodies in over thirty nations).

People, printing, and politics—all played a part in this process. Students from across Europe and Scandinavia, such as the Swedish brothers Olaus and Laurentius Petri, were drawn to Wittenberg. They participated in lively theological debates and were influenced by

Immigrants arrive at Ellis Island

Luther and his colleagues. Returning home, these students carried new gospel insight and the movement for reform. They also carried books and soon were producing more, including translations of the Bible and Luther's works into their own languages. Lutheran ideas and practices were established and endured where those gained support from powerful persons, such as Christian III. Having witnessed Luther's defense at the Diet of Worms, he introduced Lutheran reforms in his duchy in the 1520s and then into the whole of his realm when he became king of Denmark.

Lutheranism was also spread by migration as Lutherans joined in the global movements of commerce and colonization that followed the so-called age of discovery. With few, but notable, exceptions, religion was not the motivation for Lutheran migration to North America. Rather, the promise of better "daily bread" drew them from northern Europe and Scandinavia, from pre-Revolutionary time into the early twentieth century. Nonetheless, Lutheran migrants packed their Bibles, catechisms, and hymnbooks in their trunks. Upon arrival, they formed congregations, established institutions of mercy and education, and organized synods. Among the oldest congregations in the Western hemisphere is Frederick Lutheran in Charlotte Amalie on St. Thomas, Virgin Islands. Other Lutherans migrated to Australia, Brazil, Argentina, and southern Africa. In each place they adapted to unfamiliar customs, a new language, and being a minority denomination without government support.

Other Lutheran churches have their origin in missionary work begun in the early eighteenth century. Pietists' concern for holistic, personal faith generated both inner mission work close to home and the impulse to carry the

Worship in Johannesburg, South Africa

gospel to people who had not heard it. First in south India, then around the world, the Bible and the catechism, translation and schools, were among missionaries' primary evangelical tools. As the churches have matured, local Lutherans take responsibility to articulate the gospel and address their own social concerns. In the twenty-first century, these growing Lutheran churches are providing leadership to and enriching the global communion.

L. DeAne Lagerquist

ABOUT THE LUTHERANS
Lutherans in Social Service

Care for the poor and those in dire need has been a Lutheran concern from the beginning of the Reformation. In 1522, only five years after the posting of the Ninety-Five Theses, the reformers issued the Wittenberg Church Order, something of an outline for how a reshaped church community was to conduct itself. And part of that document was the call for a common or community chest—a fund that would, among other things, provide for poor orphans and children of poor people, provide refinancing of high-interest loans at 4 percent for those who were in financial trouble, and underwrite education or training for poor children. (Tellingly, Luther was challenged on the possibility of abuse, and he responded, "He who has nothing to live on should be aided. If he deceives us, what then? He must be aided again.") These ideas were soon being put into practice—not just in Wittenberg, but in other cities as far away as Strasbourg. When the pastor of St. Mary's Church in Wittenberg, Johannes Bugenhagen, became involved, the church orders also took up the cause of health care.

Theodor Fliedner

From that time on, Lutherans have keenly felt the responsibility to care for those in need, and that has been addressed in ways suitable for the time. An important step was taken by nineteenth-century German pastor Theodor Fliedner. Assigned to a poor town called Kaiserswerth (now part of Düsseldorf), he began working with inmates in the dilapidated prison there. Once he got a chaplain assigned to that prison, his focus shifted to caring for inmates, especially women, after their release. This, in turn, led to his development of a plan whereby young women would be trained to care for the sick, since there were few hospitals at that time. In 1836 he opened both a hospital and a school for training women in theology and nursing. He called these women deaconesses.

One of the graduates of that school was Mother Katinka Guldberg, who established a deaconess house in Kristiania (now Oslo), Norway, where one of her students was a young Elisabeth Fedde. After working for a time in northern Norway, Fedde moved to New York City to begin ministry there. In short order, she founded or cofounded the Norwegian Relief Society, a deaconess house, and a small hospital that eventually

Elisabeth Fedde

became the Lutheran Medical Center in Brooklyn. After a few years, she moved to Minneapolis, where again she founded a deaconess center and a hospital that has now become part of the Hennepin County Medical Center. Hospitals in Chicago and Grand Forks, North Dakota, can also be traced to her work. Other important activity in social services was propelled by Pastor William Passavant.

These days Lutheran care for the needy can readily be seen in the work of Lutheran service organizations across the country, often among the most active such agencies in any given area. Worldwide, Lutheran World Relief is known and respected not only for showing up where needed, but for staying there even after the news reports fade away. In 2015 Lutheran World Relief touched over four million people in thirty-six countries.

ABOUT THE LUTHERANS

Voices of Lutheranism: Chorales to Alabados

Situated within the wider narrative of Christian worship, the story of Lutheran music begins with Martin Luther's own gifts as a lutenist and composer. Unlike Calvin and Zwingli, who appreciated music but distrusted its emotional appeal, Luther did not want to restrict ways in which God's gifts of language and music were used in worship. In a passage that recalls the parade of voices and instruments in Psalm 150, Luther wrote that praise should "sound forth with joy" from "organs, symphonias, virginals, regals, and whatever other beloved instruments there are."

Luther singing with family and friends

Luther also knew that his fellow citizens would not be reading the scholarly documents explaining his disagreements with the Roman church. Along with his German translation of the Bible and catechisms, he wrote chorales that sought to praise and teach, placing the Word directly on the lips of the people in their own language and syntax. Aided by the expansion of printing technology, generations of authors and composers followed suit. The rhymed stanzas, catchy tunes, and dance-inspired rhythms of these chorales were not matters of happenstance but artfully combined to achieve maximum "memory" effect. (Think back: how did you learn your ABCs? By singing!) And like earlier plainchants, texts and melodies of these chorales served as building blocks for new compositions.

Luther instinctively understood the value of teamwork and cultivated partnerships with musical colleagues, inaugurating a rich tradition of collaboration between musically minded theologians (pastors) and theologically minded musicians (cantors). With Philipp Melanchthon, he established an educational model in which pastors and cantors were trained together in subjects such as grammar, rhetoric, and music. Many composers upheld as exemplars of Lutheran baroque music were products of this environment: Schütz, Praetorius, and the Bach family, to name a few.

The conditions that allowed Lutheran music to develop as it first did changed in the eighteenth century as Enlightenment ideals confronted the once-unchallenged authority of churches. As monarchies gave way to republics and democracies, composers moved from churches and courts toward concert halls. The nineteenth century saw the establishment of many civic choirs and orchestras, groups for which Mendelssohn and Brahms composed music that incorporated Lutheran chorales.

In the United States, voices of Lutheran immigrants blended with musical strands from other European denominations that had established colonial roots. The nineteenth century witnessed a constant process of intersection, recovery, and revision, allowing Anglican hymns, American shape note songs, African American spirituals, Roman plainchant, and chorales to mix freely across the frontier. Increasing ecumenical and global outlooks in the twentieth century only deepened the well of assembly song, adding familiar names like Taizé, Iona, and Hillsong to genres such as the Japanese *gagaku* and Mexican *alabados*—an abundance that Luther could hardly have imagined. Though physical materials have changed, Lutherans continue to mark days and seasons of the church year with songs from sisters and brothers of many times and places that praise, teach, pray, and bear us along our baptismal journey. Like Paul, we acclaim: Thanks be to God for this indescribable gift!

Chad Fothergill

ABOUT THE LUTHERANS

Lutheran Church Bodies in America

Family trees and lineages aren't always the most interesting reading—just try to keep your interest up as you read the first nine chapters of 1 Chronicles. On the other hand, when looking at a church body like the Evangelical Lutheran Church in America, a tracing of mergers (and divisions!) can be helpful as we learn where we came from, what issues disturbed us, and thus where we may be headed.

Hans Nielsen Hauge

The Lutheran (or evangelical) movement began, of course, in Wittenberg, Germany. And in European countries the church organizations remained relatively stable, thanks to the tradition of state churches. For a long time, the principle was *Cuius regio, eius religio*—meaning, roughly, the king gets to decide the religion. Even in the "old country," though, that began to break down in the nineteenth century as some Lutheran leaders, such as Hans Nielsen Hauge in Norway and the Saxons who would form the Lutheran Church–Missouri Synod, chafed under rules they felt violated their consciences.

When Lutherans began to arrive in the United States, they came from several countries—early on, mostly northern European and Nordic, each group affiliating with their country of origin. But Lutherans, having foresworn strong centralized control from the outset, kept thinking for themselves. Differences of opinion formed, or were inherited, over issues such as relations with Christians of differing beliefs, membership in lodges, and slavery, and theological matters such as millennialism (whether Christ will reign on

REFORMATION 500

earth for a thousand years), predestination, and ordination. So there are at least seven German groups, three Norwegian ones, and two Danish bodies, plus Swedes, Finns, Slovaks, and Icelanders, that through a series of mergers became the ELCA. A rough family tree can be seen on the other side.

Unfortunately, divisions have continued, more recently over issues like biblical inerrancy, relationships with other church bodies, ordination of women, and ordination and marriage of homosexual members. Today, even though the great majority of Lutherans in the United States belong to the ELCA, the Missouri Synod, or the Wisconsin Synod, there are more than thirty additional groups with ties to Lutheranism.

For Christians who follow the Lord who prayed that his followers might be one (John 17:11), such divisions are a cause for sorrow and repentance. The ELCA, a product of mergers, labors and prays that unity in Christ will continue to grow closer.

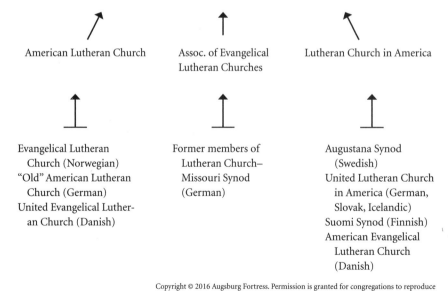

EVANGELICAL LUTHERAN CHURCH IN AMERICA

American Lutheran Church

Assoc. of Evangelical Lutheran Churches

Lutheran Church in America

Evangelical Lutheran Church (Norwegian) "Old" American Lutheran Church (German) United Evangelical Lutheran Church (Danish)

Former members of Lutheran Church–Missouri Synod (German)

Augustana Synod (Swedish) United Lutheran Church in America (German, Slovak, Icelandic) Suomi Synod (Finnish) American Evangelical Lutheran Church (Danish)

PRESERVE, SUPPORT, AND SERVE

SOME ELEMENTS FOR
A LUTHERAN THEOLOGY FOR
SOCIAL AND ECOLOGICAL
JUSTICE

A Revolutionary Theology?

The late Will Herzfeld[1] was fond of telling the story of a priest in the Philippines who, many years ago, worked among the poor and the marginalized. This priest was not afraid to denounce the abuses of the government against its own people. Eventually the priest was arrested, accused of being a communist. While in prison his kindness won him the favor of some of the guards. One day he asked a guard if he could have a little piece of bread. The guard saw no harm in it and so agreed. Then the priest asked if he could also have a little bit of wine, to which the guard also acquiesced. The priest then proceeded to celebrate the liturgy of the eucharist. His cellmate asked him if he too could partake in the sacrament, and the priest agreed. The priest continued to celebrate holy communion frequently, and the prisoners in the cell immediately adjacent to them also asked if they could share in the bread and the wine. Even though they were Muslim and not Christian, the priest agreed. Eventually, according to Herzfeld, all prisoners in that section of the prison were breaking small pieces of bread and passing it from cell to cell. Buddhists, Muslims, Christians, and others were all participating in the sacrament of the body and blood of Christ! However, soon the chief of the prison found out and became alarmed. Immediately he wrote an order for the guards. The order read as follows: "No more bread or wine for this priest. Bread and wine in the hands of this priest are dangerous revolutionary tools."

The same could have been said of Luther and the other church reformers from the sixteenth century, not only in relation to the sacraments but also in regard to the gospel. We could say that the gospel in the hands of those preachers and teachers was a dangerous revolutionary tool. Through their pen and bold proclamation the gospel did in fact revolutionize and transform the Western world from the inside out, beginning with the church and extending to social institutions such as education and the economy. The message of the gospel as proclaimed by the reformers was so powerful that even they were not able to contain it, as seen in the sad incident of Luther's furious attempt to contain the peasant's revolt even after he had supported their cause as worthy and just. The gospel was and is wildly powerful beyond anyone's control.

---

[1] Will Herzfeld was the first and so far the only African American in the United States to be bishop or president of a national Lutheran church body. He was president of the Association of Evangelical Lutheran Churches, which later merged into the Evangelical Lutheran Church in America. The story related here was told at a meeting of the former Board of the Division for Global Mission for the ELCA.

Today we desperately need to rediscover that wildly powerful revolutionary potential of the gospel that the reformers unleashed. Instead of treating our Lutheran tradition as an heirloom too precious to risk soiling by use, we must dare to use it as a tool, God's tool, to engage the crises confronting our communities and our world today, from climate change, terrorism, economic exploitation, and all forms of "-isms." Rather than treating the church as a museum of ancient yet beautiful tunes and lore, we should reconceptualize the church and the local congregation as a workshop (Luther used to call it a clinic) where God's Spirit is at work mending our broken world through the proclamation of the word, the administration of the sacraments, and concrete practices of faith active in love. Fortunately, many congregations do function as workshops of the kingdom rather than as museums of the tradition and have witnessed the power of the gospel to transform lives, to heal communities, and even to topple unjust political configurations (as was the case, for instance, in Central America during the civil war, especially in El Salvador and the mediation of the Lutheran church in the peace negotiations).

Revolutionary Elements in Lutheran Theology

The purpose of this essay is simply to draw the reader's attention to some elements of our Lutheran theological tradition that carry within them the potential of being "dangerous revolutionary tools" capable of illuminating, inspiring, or orienting the many just struggles that are going on today in the areas of social and ecological justice. We begin with the teaching that the reformers referred to as the article by which the church stands or falls, namely, justification by grace through faith.

THE PRIORITY OF GRACE

The heart of the gospel and what makes it so wildly powerful is the proclamation that "God, who is rich in mercy, out of the great love with which he loved us even when we were dead through our trespasses, made us alive together with Christ—by grace you have been saved" (Eph. 2:4-5). In the realm of everyday life, this translates into an affirmation of the worth and dignity of the human being regardless of socioeconomic status, racial or ethnic identification, sexual orientation, or physical or mental ability or disability. The intrinsic dignity of the human being is anchored in nothing less than God and the irrevocable act performed by Christ on the cross on behalf of all humanity.

A parental tenderness in the heart of God is revealed in Christ. To see oneself reflected in the mirror of that divine heart, exposed on the cross, is a life-changing experience. This is extremely important. A shortcoming with many activist groups engaged in just struggles for social transformation is that the necessarily urgent emphasis on changing unjust socioeconomic or political structures indirectly implies postponing the happiness (for lack of a better word) of those suffering under such structures until after the struggle has become successful. What is so powerful about the promise of the gospel is that it is available here and now. The gospel has the power to make a pauper feel like a king even while still poor. It also has the power to make the rich feel like a beggar who has been invited to a feast. And it makes them both realize their true kinship and responsibility for each other. In the end the well-being of one is inextricably bound to the well-being of the other (not as rich and poor but simply as two human beings in need of God's grace).

However, there are two dangerous distortions of the Lutheran emphasis on the priority of God's grace that need to be addressed. The first one is quietism, and the second one, to be discussed in the next section, is the cheapening of grace. It is easy to mistakenly assume that if grace is available to all regardless of social or economic status, then a person's circumstances in life (whether the person is poor or in situations of oppression and abuse) don't matter. Therefore, the church should stay away from politics or social justice movements. The irony in this position is that if the reformers had practiced it, the Reformation never would have happened! The signing of the Augsburg Confession was as much a political event as an ecclesiastical affair. Furthermore, Luther was never shy to remind the rulers of his day, with colorful language, of their God-given responsibility to look after the well-being of their subjects. He even proposed concrete social reforms, such as making education available to girls, keeping a communal chest to aid the poor, and prohibiting the practice of usury. The key for the reformers was that works of social engagement or reform had to be motivated by love (or more accurately, by obedience to God's command to love the neighbor). What had to be avoided at all cost was the idea that by engaging in that type of work one was earning merit with God. Also to be avoided was the identification of any social structure (e.g., state, church, or commune) with the kingdom of God. The kingdom of God always remains as a transcendental point of reference that judges all the concrete historical kingdoms, governments, and institutions of this world. It never becomes realized in history except as eschatological horizon.

When we have been awakened to the fact of God's grace, we find ourselves solidly anchored to the immutable promises of the everlasting God. Only then do we experience God as a mighty fortress, as did Luther and the psalmist before him—not a fortress from whence to escape or hide from the world but rather a place from whence to courageously engage the world moved by love and inspired by faith and hope. Furthermore, when we are anchored in grace, we are also able to see the foolishness of seeking happiness in anything other than God, from the accumulation of wealth or power to the pursuit of beauty or success. This is important in the context of struggles for social and ecological justice because unjust social arrangements are hegemonically sustained in great part by the voluntary participation of people exploited by those very systems, who are motivated by the false belief that the solution to their existential dilemmas can be offered only by the system. This can be seen, for example, in the case of the lottery, to which many people (especially poor people) sacrifice thousands of dollars in their lifetimes, moved by the dual false promise that they could end up as millionaires and that being a millionaire will solve their existential problems. In the end it doesn't work that way. Thus, the gospel can awaken people to the ways in which unjust social arrangements feed on what the reformers called our concupiscence, the insatiable hunger of the self for things that it thinks can satisfy it (including money, sex, power, fame, and even saintliness).

THE BONDAGE OF THE WILL AND THE THOROUGH CORRUPTION OF THE HUMAN BEING

Another potentially revolutionary element in Lutheran theology is its emphasis on how thoroughly corrupt human beings (and institutions) are as a consequence of sin. Sin is not a stain on the human soul but a corruption that has disfigured the very image in which God had created us. This corruption is so deep that it not only affects our moral behavior but also distorts our capacity to will and even to reason. Against the optimism of the humanists of his day who proclaimed the freedom of the will, such as Erasmus of Rotterdam, Luther preached instead the bondage of the will. According to the reformer, even our good deeds and well-meaning efforts are ultimately sin. Because of sin, even our acts of love and kindness are secretly (and often unconsciously) motivated by our concupiscence. I love because I want to be loved; I help others because I want to be regarded as good; I can even sacrifice my life for a just cause and yet be motivated by the hunger of the self to be praised or at least accepted as good (see 1 Cor. 13:3). The human mind is also affected by this corruption, so that instead of perceiving things as they are, it will see them according to its own desires and needs. In fact, Luther's own view of reason was that it existed in the tension between being a gift from God and yet also being always ready to go to be with whoever would offer it satisfaction. (Luther's language was more direct, of course.) So from a Lutheran perspective, neither theology nor science is beyond the distorting effects of sin. Our view of reality, our theories and theologies, are always as captive to sin as we are.

Ironically, that pessimistic (others would say, realistic) understanding of the human being can be a very powerful resource for the struggle for social and ecological justice. We don't have to wait until we are pure or innocent before we can engage in the practice of justice. There is no privileged place outside the sinful structures that we are fighting from within which we can confront those structures. The truth is that even as we engage in the sincere prophetic denunciation of unjust structures and practices, and engage in the practice of reforming or even dismantling them, we are aware of the fact that we too are complicit in those same structures, practices, or systems. For instance, even as I engage in advocacy for the rights of refugees and immigrants, the way the global system is set up means that that same injustice that I am fighting makes it possible for me and my allies to have cheap goods available, such as clothing, food, and electronics, even the same resources I use to fight that injustice. Why is this liberating? Because it frees us from the compulsion to act out of a need to assuage our sense of guilt rather than out of a genuine concern for the well-being of the other. When we delude ourselves, thinking that there is a space of innocence or purity, then the unconscious criteria and motivation for our actions are not whether they truly result in the well-being of the other but, rather, whether they make me feel righteous and good about myself. Thus many well-intentioned activists or allies get fooled into unknowingly perpetuating the same system they are fighting because it allows them to sort of blow off the socioemotional steam (anger, outrage, indignation, empathy, compassion) that could otherwise be used to dismantle it and truly change it.

Rather than acting out of a sense of (or desire for) self-righteousness, we are liberated by the gospel to act boldly even as we are aware that we might be wrong and that our actions are in fact sinful. This is a truth that was articulated beautifully by that famous German pastor, theologian, and martyr, Dietrich Bonhoeffer. Writing from behind bars as a consequence of his own involvement in the resistance against the Nazi regime, and reflecting on what he had learned from such an experience, he wrote, "Civil courage . . . can grow only out of the free responsibility of free man [and woman]. . . . It depends on a God who demands responsible action in a bold venture of faith, and who promises forgiveness and consolation to the man [and woman] who becomes a sinner in that venture."[2] And later on he said: "I believe that even our mistakes and shortcomings are turned to good account, and that it is no harder for God to deal with them than with our supposedly good deeds. I believe that God is no timeless fate, but that he waits for and answers sincere prayers and responsible actions."[3] This should not be confused with the idea that "the end justifies the means." The truth is that the means must correspond with the end or else the end itself is betrayed and what is achieved is something very different from the ideal that was used to justify the means. Love must always be the ultimate criterion of both the means and the ends. But only the one who is sincerely aware of his or her own inescapable guilt and of the grace by which God has accepted him or her even while being unacceptable can truly act freely for the sake of the well-being of the other. As Christ puts it: "The one to whom little is forgiven, loves little" (Luke 7:47).

2   Dietrich Bonhoeffer, *Letters and Papers from Prison* (New York: Simon & Schuster, 1971), 6.
3   Ibid., 11.

The tendency exists among some activist groups to draw a Manichean line in the sand and divide the world into us (the righteous fighters for justice) versus them (the evil minions of the corrupt system). As a strategy for community organizing, that approach is understandable because it helps create group cohesiveness against a clear and unambiguous common enemy that must be defeated. The problem with this approach is that it risks inoculating activists or social justice fighters from the ways in which they too participate and benefit from unjust systems. Thus revolutions easily turn into dictatorships, and activists intensely committed to racial justice might also be unconscious perpetuators of other forms of injustice. The awareness of the bondage of the will and of the thorough corruption of the human being and of human institutions call for an attitude of humility and daily repentance. It also calls for authentic dialogue, because sin is universal but not undifferentiated; therefore the neighbor who is radically other from me might be able to see certain expressions of my sin that I myself am unaware of. And vice versa, I can see some of the blind spots in my neighbor that he or she is probably unaware of. The purpose of these remarks is not to disparage the important and very hard work being done by activists on the ground but rather to offer them an alternative way of seeing things that might be helpful for their struggle.

THE ESCHATOLOGICAL HORIZON OF HOPE

A corollary of the Lutheran emphasis on the thorough corruption of the human being and of human institutions is that no state, church, or political, economic, or social system can be equated with the kingdom of God. The kingdom (or kin-dom) is the eschatological horizon (*telos*) of the creative and redemptive work of God. However, similar to the horizon (or to an asymptote in mathematics), it can never be reached, even as it inspires us to journey toward it. In the language of the scriptures, we don't go to the kingdom; the kingdom comes to us. Hence the prayer: "Your kingdom come."

The glimpses of the kingdom of God displayed by Jesus can offer us a criterion to judge all social, economic, political, and cultural institutions from the perspective of faith. The criterion is not whether an institution directly utilizes the teachings and symbols of the Christian faith (such as the Ten Commandments, the Sermon on the Mount, the cross, or the nativity scene). The question is whether its general thrust and effects are in tandem with or in opposition to the general thrust and orientation of the kingdom of God as revealed in Christ. Because from the perspective of faith God is believed to be the ultimate ruler of the world, and not just the ruler of the believer's individual life or of one's religion only, the claims of God are universal in scope. The caveat, again, is that because of the distorting effects of sin, no person or social institution or movement has unambiguous access to such understanding. Even the gospel texts have been written by very fallible human beings whose understanding of Christ, though illuminated by the Holy Spirit, continued to be marred by sin (as made clear in the scriptures themselves!).

Without an objective criterion for justice, the various social and ecological struggles for justice can become easily relativized and robbed of their effectiveness. If there is no objective criterion, as ambiguous as it may be, then the struggle becomes a game of tug-of-war, and whichever group has the greatest social capital or power gets to define what is good and desirable even at the expense of other vulnerable groups. That is why the gospel (and other religious traditions such as Islam in the case of Malcolm X) has played a central role in the struggles of liberation by those coming from impoverished and marginalized communities. An example that comes to mind is the singing of spirituals and the centrality of preaching in the civil rights struggle. The kingdom of God anchors the struggle for justice in the unshakable rock of God and God's purposes. That is what allowed a simple monk armed with nothing else but the conviction of the gospel to challenge the most powerful institutions of his times, the church and the empire—and win!

Conclusion

The gospel, in the hands of men and women of conviction, with a burning desire for the healing of society and of the planet, can indeed be a powerful revolutionary tool. There are many more elements in the Lutheran tradition that can be very helpful in the struggle for ecological and social wholesomeness. It is up to us to pick them up and dare to engage in the difficult work to which God has called us. It is up to us to be a church that is a workshop rather than a museum, not a monument to a beautiful tradition but a clinic where a broken society and a broken planet can still find healing.

Some General Suggestions for Congregations That Want to Engage in the Practice of Social or Ecological Justice

Listen

Don Quixote was famous for rushing to the rescue of people in need only to leave them worse than they were before! Before rushing into concrete actions, we must take the time to listen to the situation. One listens by doing the following:

- Talking to those directly affected
- Talking to those who have been doing the same work long before us
- Using the best tools at our disposal to analyze the situation

Never stop listening to the people or communities most directly affected by the issue you have been called to address.

Put in place systems to help you receive honest input regarding the real effects of your efforts on the ground.

Find ways to objectively assess the effectiveness with which the goal has been met.

Pray

Before his "Here I Stand" at Worms, Luther spent the night on his knees praying. Why is prayer so important?

- Prayer reminds us whose work it is that we are about.
- Prayer empties us of the quixotic compulsion to rush into action at the wrong time. Remember Jesus' words: "Suppose one of you wants to build a tower. Won't you first sit down and estimate the cost to see if you have enough money to complete it? For if you lay the foundation and are not able to finish it, everyone who sees it will ridicule you, saying, 'This person began to build and wasn't able to finish'" (Luke 14:28-30 NIV).
- Prayer reminds us of our weakness through which God works wonders (see 2 Cor. 12:9). Thus prayer protects us from the temptation to seek power as a prerequisite to achieve the good. That is the beginning of corruption.

Know Yourself

What gifts and talents has God blessed this community with?

How can we pair the gifts of the community with the problem or need we are trying to address?

What are unhealthy tendencies in the community that should be kept in check?

Know Your Goal

There is a joke about an airplane pilot who announces to his passengers: "The good news is that we are going as fast as we can. The bad news is that we don't know if we are heading in the right direction." You should know your goal.

Don't underestimate the motivational power of a clear sense of direction and purpose.

Break down the problem you have been called to address into its smaller components and choose the one that fits with the interests, skills, and resources of your congregation. For example, global warming is overwhelming, but addressing the lack of trees in a local neighborhood or advocating for the use of non-carbon-based energy alternatives at the county or city level is feasible. One goal leads to the next.

Know Your Partners

When the prophet Elijah complained bitterly that he was the only one remaining who was faithful to the God of Israel, he was told by God that there were in fact seven thousand more who were also faithful (1 Kings 19:18). We are not alone. It is very likely that there are other groups, institutions, or individuals who are equally passionate and committed to the same goal that you have been called to pursue. Look for them.

Rather than starting from scratch, it might be helpful to join a movement or organization that already exists and that has experience and a good track record in addressing the issue that your congregation has been called to address.

Consider forming a coalition with other churches or organizations. Ecumenical and interreligious movements have a greater force of persuasion. Additionally, they are more likely to receive grants for their efforts than single organizations.

Celebrate the Small Victories

Social and ecological justice work can be deflating and exhausting because the issues are so overwhelming and the situation is often very dire. So it is important to take the time to pause and celebrate even small achievements.

Take the time to share with your partners and donors the small victories. They are glimmers of light in the midst of the night; they remind us that the status quo is not the only possibility.

Always thank those who helped, and make them feel that the victory is theirs as well. That will help keep them motivated when defeat comes.

Learn from Failure

I recently heard a martial arts instructor say, "Just because you failed doesn't mean that it is over!" Keep that in mind; you will need it a lot.

Defeats will be more abundant than victories, but they can teach us a lot about what doesn't work and how to proceed next time.

Keep Bonhoeffer's words near: "I believe that even our mistakes and shortcomings are turned to good account, and that it is no harder for God to deal with them than with our supposedly good deeds."[4]

Carmelo Santos

---

4   Ibid.

AN ECO-JUSTICE REFORMATION FOR 2017 AND BEYOND

Many Lutherans are committed to fostering an ongoing reformation that incorporates ecological justice into the full life, identity, and mission of the Evangelical Lutheran Church in America. There is now an "Eco-Justice Reformation 2017 Working Group," an informal group of more than fifty pastors, teachers, and laity, calling for the church to address more fully the ecological crises facing creation.

The seeds of the resources needed for such a reformation are rooted in our Reformation traditions. We are called by scripture to serve and keep the earth, enjoined by our theological roots to honor God the creator, and led by a theology of the cross to seek justice in solidarity with the most vulnerable humans and now also with our most vulnerable fellow creatures.

The church can rise to this great work of our time with grace and love by renewing our worship, our theology, our ethics, and our spirituality to embrace God's deep and abiding love for the whole creation and by reclaiming our human relationship with all of life.

The following are among the resources developed by the Working Group and available at http://www. lutheransrestoringcreation.org/500th-anniversary-of-the-reformation.

Lutheran Foundations for an Eco-Reformation
- **Online Theological Resources:** Articles, lectures, videos, sermons.
- **Resources to be Published:** *Eco-Reformation: Grace and Hope for a Planet in Peril* (Wipf and Stock, 2016); issues on eco-reformation in *Currents in Theology and Mission*; *Dialog*; and the *Journal of Lutheran Ethics*; and some adult study guides.
- **Speaker Bureau for 2016–17 Events:** Profiles of twenty outstanding leaders available to address ecological reformation topics at synod assemblies, professional leadership conferences, and congregational lecture series.
- **Earthbound (Six-Part Video Series):** *Created and Called to Care for Creation* is available at a special discount for 2016–17.

Educational Materials
- **Luther's Small Catechism:** revised with questions and actions by an ELCA pastor to incorporate creation care into instruction for youth and adults.

- **Luther Quotations:** A PowerPoint presentation of quotations relevant to creation care from the writings of Martin Luther.
- **Lutheran Study Guide to Pope Francis's Encyclical *Laudato si':*** A four-week study for congregational, college, and seminary classes. It takes up the theme of the 500th anniversary.

Worship and Preaching

- **Creation-Care Worship:** Resources for worship to encompass ecological justice throughout the church year as we observe the 2017 anniversary, including materials to celebrate an optional four-week Season of Creation.
- **Eco-Justice Preaching:** Fresh care-for-creation reflections on the lessons for every Sunday, along with a special challenge to preach creation care on Reformation Sunday.

Synod Resources

- **Green Events:** Comprehensive guidelines to plan and carry out anniversary events that are ecologically responsible.
- **Resolutions:** An extensive collection of synod resolutions memorializing an eco-reformation of the church, addressing climate change, and calling for reinvestment.

We are urging the development of resources in synods, seminaries, colleges, camps, and congregations that foster an eco-justice reformation of the ELCA on the occasion of the 500th anniversary of the Reformation. We invite you to join us.

David Rhoads for Lutherans Restoring Creation. www.lutheransrestoringcreation.org.

LIVING OUT THE SMALL CATECHISM

Most of us think of the Small Catechism as something to be memorized that teaches us how to understand life with God and other people. And it is that. But what if we put a more active spin on the catechism? What if we looked to it to inspire concrete actions we might take, thereby expressing its wisdom in positive deeds, not just words? That's what we will explore here. (If you don't have a Small Catechism handy, it is included in *Evangelical Lutheran Worship*, pages 1160–67, or it can be ordered from augsburgfortress.org.)

The Small Catechism has six chief parts:
- The Ten Commandments
- The Apostles' Creed
- The Lord's Prayer
- Holy Baptism
- Confession
- Holy Communion, or the Sacrament of the Altar

Of those, the last three are in a different category, more purely gifts of God and perhaps less adaptable to being spun out in deeds of service. So we will focus on the first three. Where might each of those lead us? Please keep in mind that this isn't meant to be an exhaustive list but rather something to seed your own imagination.

The Ten Commandments

Commandments tell us what to do, or more often what not to do. Luther's commentary opens up these narrow strictures and leads us toward ideas for positive action.

1. You shall have no other gods.

   Explore other faiths, such as Judaism, Islam, Hinduism. Doing so need not threaten our own Christian beliefs, but will help strengthen understanding of their perspectives on God, create partnerships, and reduce harmful stereotypes. Read about them in a resource such as *Honoring Our Neighbor's Faith* (Augsburg Fortress), invite speakers from or about other traditions, visit their places of worship.

2. You shall not make wrongful use of the name of the Lord your God.

   Get creative about prayer! One ELCA pastor has sat in a coffee shop with a FREE PRAYER sign. Let people know you are willing to pray for their concerns. Start a prayer ministry in your congregation. Work to make the intercessory prayers in your worship more tailored to your assembly, more eloquent.

3. Remember the sabbath day, and keep it holy.
    In many places, a struggle for parents of children and youth is athletics that schedule games and matches on Sunday mornings. If this is the case where you live, consider joining with other area churches to lobby for fewer (or better, no) games before noon on Sundays.

4. Honor your father and your mother.
    Many church buildings are underused on weekdays. Even if you don't have a daily preschool program, your building can be a gift to parents in many ways. Perhaps you could have a staffed nursery near a Wi-Fi-equipped room where parents can work, or an arrangement for child care while single parents get away for shopping, appointments, or recreation. Check about local requirements for staffing and insurance.

5. You shall not murder.
    Who are the most vulnerable in your city or town, and how can you support them? Some ideas would include donating to or volunteering at a shelter for battered women, providing gym space for at-risk youth in afternoons and evenings, participating in a program that provides meals for seniors, tutoring recent immigrants.

6. You shall not commit adultery.
    Our society's unrealistic views on marriage often mean that once the wedding is over, young couples struggle to establish sustainable relationships. Brainstorm how your congregation might help: support groups, topics and discussions, mentors, people to call when problems arise.

7. You shall not steal.
    The poorest among us are often most vulnerable to predatory lending practices such as payday loans. Using the enticements of readily available cash, victims are immersed ever more deeply in debt. Study the issue and find out how you can help influence legislators crack down on the practice.

8. You shall not bear false witness against your neighbor.
    The saying goes "If it sounds too good to be true, it probably is." Often the reverse is also true: people and groups get an undeserved bad rap. This can be countered on an individual basis by speaking up when you hear slander, or through a congregation coming to the aid of a population denigrated because of race, ethnic or religious identity, or economic class.

9. You shall not covet your neighbor's house.
    When it comes to property care, homeowners or renters can get overwhelmed when visited by illness, injury, or the frailty of old age. How can you be of assistance? Cleaning, painting, lawn care, and simple maintenance are examples of helpful activities that can be taken on by youth or adult groups or individuals.

10. You shall not covet your neighbor's wife, or male or female slave, or ox, or donkey, or anything that belongs to your neighbor.

The book of Acts tells us that the early church held everything in common. That may not be practical these days, but what about a decentralized "lending library" of tools? Whether it's cooking, home maintenance, lawn and garden—each area has specialized tools that aren't needed very often. Consider creating an online listing of items that people would be willing to loan out within the congregation.

The Apostles' Creed

This ancient confession of who we understand God to be is divided into three parts, or articles, each highlighting a different aspect of God's work on our behalf. And each can suggest different sorts of learnings and activities.

- First Article—God the Father—On Creation

  Organize or take part in activities to clean up your local environment, such as picking up trash along nearby waterways. Are there organizations working to reclaim good food that restaurants and stores no longer want? If so, get involved! If not, how can you help start such a project? Watch for signs that vulnerable neighbors need help getting proper health care—a ride to the doctor, even maybe staying with them during the appointment, can be life-saving.

- Second Article—Jesus Christ—On Redemption

  Once we leave the worship space at church and move into the adult forum classroom, we may often encounter topics such as recycling or the latest fiction, but more rarely learning experiences around redemption or salvation. Don't forget to provide opportunities for interested people (from within or without) to find out more about Christ's work. David Lose's *Making Sense of the Cross* (Augsburg Fortress) is one among many good resources.

- Third Article—the Holy Spirit—On Being Made Holy

  The Holy Spirit gathers, but we are welcome to lend a hand. Take the pulse of your neighborhood—what sorts of social events might appeal to that population? What might they fear from coming to a church? How can you help them to overcome those fears? The object is not to trick people, simply to welcome them.

The Lord's Prayer

This most beloved of prayers gathers many concerns that are central to our life as Christians, and so its petitions and Luther's explanations of them provide another outline for ways we can be of service to others.

- Introduction: Our Father in heaven.

  Children need a safe place where they can "ask boldly." We hope they have that with their parent or parents, but how wonderful if they also have such trusting relationships with pastors and members at church. Think of one or two children in your congregation—how can you (with appropriate boundaries) foster such a relationship?

1. Hallowed be your name.

   Old-timers may remember Jim Croce's song "I've Got a Name." God knows each baptized child (however old) by name. A "My Name Project" could help lift up the name and identity of children and adults. On index cards, put the name, its meaning if known, and why they received that name. The cards could be incorporated into a festival of baptismal remembrance.

2. Your kingdom come.
    The concept of the kingdom of God is a deep and broad one, good fodder for a Bible study. It has picked up varying nuances in different times. And it was a key concept for Martin Luther. Because of that, it would be worthwhile to turn to this same petition in the Large Catechism (*Book of Concord*, p. 446). Less than two pages long, this is well worth reading and discussing.

3. Your will be done, on earth as in heaven.
    Here is a subject for study and for action: What is God's will in today's world? Think about "hot button" issues like immigration, welfare, abortion, child wellness, equal justice, and many more. Study what the Bible says, particularly the New Testament. Then—you are the church! Make your voices heard.

4. Give us today our daily bread.
    Luther's extensive list of what "daily bread" includes is good for us to remember as we work and pray. But a good start would be to go with the obvious meaning and help the organization Bread for the World. Go to bread.org and look under "Get Involved." Or, for a Lutheran option, consider Lutheran World Relief (lwr.org).

5. Forgive us our sins as we forgive those who sin against us.
    Forgiveness is hard for everyone. It's important that the church, and the Christians who form it, lead the way, and forgive both on an individual and on a larger level. What groups are "the enemy" these days? How can we live out forgiveness toward them?

6. Save us from the time of trial.
    Trials and testings come in many forms, but in this time and place, few are as threatening as the forces of consumerism. Powerful voices and images tell us that what we really need is to accumulate more *stuff*. Yet a witness to a simpler life can be very attractive too. Clothing drives, soup suppers, community-oriented recreation—all these can speak eloquently.

7. And deliver us from evil.
    Evil can erupt from any corner of society, and while we ultimately look to God for protection, we can also be God's hands in this regard. While we must not blindly vilify any group (for instance, neither people of color nor the police), we can speak up in favor of equal protections and uphold those who conscientiously work to protect.

•   Conclusion: For the kingdom, the power, and the glory are yours, now and forever. Amen.
    As we consider service projects—"works" that we may do—we remember that as beneficial as those may be, finally it is God's grace that is our source of all good things.

PLAN, EXPLORE, AND PUBLICIZE

ORGANIZING YOUR
REFORMATION OBSERVANCE
A Checklist

Congregations that observe their own anniversaries know that it takes time to plan. They often start a year or more ahead of time. And they often plan activities and communications spanning a year's time. Although the 500th anniversary date itself falls in October 2017, it's not too early to begin planning how you will bring life to this observance in a way that's suitable to your context. Here is a checklist of tasks, ideas, and questions to get you started.

Organizing your Reformation observance

- Identify a group of leaders to carry this task forward. What areas of congregational life will be included? Worship and music, learning and teaching, service and public witness, hospitality and welcome are some of the areas most congregations would consider.
- Who will make up this group? If your events and activities are to be not just backward- but forward-looking, consider including people of a variety of ages and especially young people, who will carry the gifts of the Reformation into the next five hundred years. Think not only of people who have deep roots in the Lutheran Church but also those who are new to this expression of Christianity.
- Could your planning group include also a guest or two from outside your congregation, such as a representative from a local Roman Catholic parish or from a congregation of one of the ELCA's full communion partners? After all, this anniversary belongs to the whole church and not just to Lutherans, and it offers a great opportunity to connect with other Christians about where we all have come since 1517.
- Once your group is assembled, identify the goals and hoped-for outcomes for this anniversary in your setting. Be realistic and mindful of your capacities and the reality that this observance will best enhance your ongoing mission and ministry rather than distract from it.
- In advance of your first meeting, order or download selected resources that you will ask your working group to read and reflect on. In addition to this sourcebook and the resources it highlights, even more resource ideas can be reviewed by exploring the designated websites for the ELCA and Augsburg Fortress.
- Identify the time frame for your observance. Will it be the church year beginning with Advent 2016? One year, from Reformation 2016 to Reformation 2017? Only the fall of 2017? This decision will help you determine the scope for which you are planning.
- Begin to sketch out events and activities in one or more of the following categories or others you may think of.

Worship and music

- Will Reformation emphases be woven into regular Sunday worship throughout the time frame of your observance? Or will you plan mainly for a given month, or just a Sunday in 2017?
- How will music enliven your observance? Will you learn hymns and songs, whether new or from the heritage? What might challenge and delight your choirs or other ensembles? Will you plan a hymn/music festival?
- Will you incorporate a Reformation-related worship series for Wednesdays in Lent 2017 or at another time?
- Will you join voices with other Christians in an event designed for ecumenical participation? Be sure to allow plenty of time to plan graciously with your neighbors for such an occasion.

Learning and teaching

- Gather information and samples of resources to explore for use with adults and youth. Select one or more (or design your own) that seem most promising for your setting.
- Consider approaches designed for conversation with people from other Christian traditions. Although such conversations involve careful thought and planning, they can enrich understanding and expand awareness of the Spirit's gift of unity.
- How will the stories and insights of the Reformation become a part of your regular offerings for young people preparing for affirmation of baptism?
- How will your children learn the story of God's love also through the stories of key people and events in the Reformation narrative?
- Could one or more intergenerational events be a part of your planning?

Service and public witness

- How will your congregation participate in "God's work. Our hands"? Worship together with others across the ELCA on September 11, 2016, and September 10, 2017?
- How can you partner with Lutheran service and advocacy groups near you or at the national/global level to lift up and extend the work we do together to serve our neighbors, to care for creation, and to seek justice and peace throughout the earth?
- How can you prepare to communicate effectively to people in your community during the anniversary year when there is likely to be media interest in the questions "Who are the Lutherans? What's their story?"

Hospitality and welcome

- These important dimensions of congregational life often accompany events and activities such as those described above. In addition to the ways food and festive fellowship may be a part of your congregation's gatherings, planning a gracious welcome for visitors and ecumenical guests will take on special importance.
- Lutherans in North America have often been identified with certain cultural markers, from brats to lutefisk to Lake Wobegon. Hospitality plans can certainly include an aspect of fun and local tradition. But consider also how to lift up the Lutheran emphasis of the wide welcome of God's grace and mercy that transcends narrow—and sometimes outdated—cultural characteristics in order to embrace the whole world and its peoples.

FOR FURTHER EXPLORATION

As the 500th anniversary of the Reformation draws near, a wealth of resources is appearing. Some of these are described elsewhere in this sourcebook, but here are some resources and websites worth looking into.

Books

Together by Grace: Introducing the Lutherans
    Edited by Kathryn Kleinhans. Available at augsburgfortress.org.
Together by Grace serves as a rich resource for getting to know who Lutherans are, what they teach, where they come from, and where they are today. It includes sections on Lutheran basics, Lutheran history and practice, and a wide range of stories from the global Lutheran family. *Together by Grace* can be read by individuals, or each section can be used as a session for small or large group studies. A leader guide will be available as a digital download.

Papa Luther: A Graphic Novel
    By Daniel J. Maurer. Illustrated by Caitlin Like. Available at augsburgfortress.org.
Papa Luther is an 80-page, full-color graphic novel—or comic book—for children ages 8 to 12, and is also suitable for older youth (and more than a few adults too!). The book tells the story of Martin Luther and the Reformation as seen through the eyes of his children. Perfect for individual reading, as well as in small or large group studies. A leader guide will be available as a digital download.

Luther's Small Catechism anniversary editions
    Available at augsburgfortress.org.
Luther's Small Catechism is presented in three editions to mark the observance of 500 years of the Reformation era beginning in 1517 and to support the ELCA's catechism initiative in 2016–2017: a Study Edition with a new introduction by Timothy J. Wengert, new illustrations by Gertrud Mueller Nelson, notes, and supplementary content; a Pocket Edition containing the basic text; and a newly developed catechism mobile app, available through the principal app stores.

Declaration on the Way: Church, Ministry, and Eucharist
    Developed as a resource by the ecumenical offices of the ELCA and the U.S. Conference of Catholic Bishops. Available at augsburgfortress.org.
Declaration on the Way celebrates fifty years of international and regional Lutheran–Catholic dialogues and harvests the results of those efforts into Statements of Agreement on church, ministry, and eucharist. It invites both communions to affirm the unity achieved through these agreements and establish

church practices that reflect this growth. Read and discuss Declaration on the Way in adult study groups, affirm and celebrate these Lutheran–Catholic agreements, and take steps toward greater unity in your neighborhood or community.

One Hope: Re-Membering the Body of Christ

By Julie K. Aageson, John Borelli, John Klassen, Derek R. Nelson, Martha Stortz, Jessica Wrobleski. Available at augsburgfortress.org.

One Hope: Re-Membering the Body of Christ is a rich ecumenical resource designed to help Catholic and Lutheran communities mark the approaching 500th anniversary of the Reformation. By gathering together to reflect on and discuss its contents, Christians will foster the church's unity on a grassroots level and grow in their awareness of the ways that unity already exists. The essays in One Hope are the product of an intense collaborative process by six gifted scholars and pastoral leaders, three Lutheran and three Catholic.

From Conflict to Communion

Available at ELCA500.org and lutheranworld.org.

The Lutheran–Roman Catholic Commission on Unity invites all Christians to study its report and to walk along the path toward the full, visible unity of the church. Free, downloadable document and study guide available.

Martin Luther's Ninety-Five Theses: With Introduction, Commentary, and Study Guide

By Timothy J. Wengert. Available at augsburgfortress.org.

By almost any reckoning, the Ninety-Five Theses ranks as the most important text of the Reformation, if not in substance at least in impact. This new translation is accompanied by two related and essential documents: Luther's Letter to Archbishop Albrecht of Mainz and his 1518 Sermon on Indulgences.

The Annotated Luther, Volume 1: The Roots of Reform

Edited by Timothy J. Wengert. Available at augsburgfortress.org.

Writings that defined the roots of reform set in motion by Martin Luther, beginning with the Ninety-Five Theses (1517) through The Freedom of a Christian (1520).

The Annotated Luther, Volume 2: Word and Faith

Edited by Kirsi I. Stjerna. Available at augsburgfortress.org.

A number of the writings categorized under the theme Word and Faith. Luther was particularly focused on what the word "does" in order to create and sustain faith.

The Annotated Luther, Volume 3: Church and Sacraments

Edited by Paul W. Robinson. Available at augsburgfortress.org.

Five key writings that focus on Martin Luther's understanding of the gospel as it relates to church, sacraments, and worship. Included in the volume are The Babylonian Captivity of the Church (1520); The German Mass and Order of the Liturgy (1526); That These Words of Christ, "This is my Body," etc., Still Stand Firm against the Fanatics (1527); Concerning Rebaptism (1528); and On the Councils and the Church (1539).

The Annotated Luther, Volume 4: Pastoral Writings
   Edited by Mary Jane Haemig. Available at augsburgfortress.org.
Presents an array of Martin Luther's writings related to pastoral work, including sermons, hymns, letters, writings on prayer and the Christian life, as well as his widely used Small Catechism.

The Annotated Luther, Volume 5: Christian Life in the World
   Edited by Hans J. Hillerbrand. Available at augsburgfortress.org.
Features Luther's writings that intersect church and state, faith, and life lived as a follower of Christ. His insights regarding marriage, trade, public education, and war are articulated. His theological and biblical insights also colored the way he spoke of the "Jews" and "Turks," as well his admonition to the German peasants in their uprisings against the established powers.

The Annotated Luther, Volume 6: The Interpretation of Scripture
   Edited by Euan K. Cameron. Available at augsburgfortress.org.
Features Luther the exegete and Bible teacher. His vast exegetical writings and lectures on scripture are narrowed to some of the most important samples from both the Old and New Testaments. Also includes his insights regarding Bible translating in *On Translating*.

Also available at augsburgfortress.org: The Annotated Luther Study Editions of key writings by Luther. These compact offprints from the larger volumes are ideal for students, scholars, and general readers. The first volumes include *The Freedom of the Christian*, *Treatise on Good Works*, and *The Large Catechism*.

Luther the Reformer: The Story of the Man and His Career, Revised Edition
   James Kittelson; revised and updated by Hans H. Wiersma. Available at augsburgfortress.org.
For nearly thirty years, *Luther the Reformer* has been the standard Luther biography. Fair, insightful, and detailed without being overwhelming, Kittelson was able to negotiate a "middle way" that presented a complete chronological picture of Luther. Now Hans H. Wiersma gives us a revision in which the research is updated and the text is revised throughout.

Resilient Reformer: The Life and Thought of Martin Luther
   By Timothy F. Lull and Derek R. Nelson. Available at augsburgfortress.org.
In this telling, Luther is an energetic, resilient actor, driven by very human strengths and failings, always wishing to do right by his understanding of God and the witness of the scriptures.

When Lightning Struck! The Story of Martin Luther
   By Danika Cooley. Available at augsburgfortress.org.
In this fast-paced, action-packed novel of Martin Luther's life, Danika Cooley conveys both the drama and the meaning of the Reformation for teens and younger readers like no one before her!

Atlas of the European Reformations
   By Tim Dowley. Available at augsburgfortress.org.
A new atlas of the European Reformations has been keenly needed. Featuring more than sixty brand-new maps, graphics, and timelines, the atlas is a valuable companion to any study of the Reformation era and is written for readers at any level.

Gift and Promise: The Augsburg Confession and the Heart of Christian Theology
>   By Edward H. Schroeder. Available at augsburgfortress.org.

Gift and Promise shows that the theology of the Augsburg Confession is a gift for the world today. This volume establishes the "hub" of the Augsburg Confession—justification by faith alone—which is traced to its source in Luther's theology of the cross.

Book of Harmony: Spirit and Service in the Lutheran Confessions
>   By Martin J. Lohrmann. Available at augsburgfortress.org.

This study presents the Lutheran Confessions as a valuable partner for ministry in twenty-first-century contexts, interpreting these teachings for those who want to learn more about this branch of the Reformation.

Martin Luther and the Called Life
>   By Mark D. Tranvik. Available at augsburgfortress.org.

One of the hallmarks of Luther's theology was its concern for daily life. The author turns attention to the importance of vocation in Luther's life and in doing so discovers renewed insights into this important theme. Vocation, the called life, is a way of understanding that all of life is under the care and interest of God.

Engaging Others, Knowing Ourselves: A Lutheran Calling in a Multi-Religious World
>   Developed by ELCA Consultative Panels on Lutheran–Jewish and Lutheran–Muslim Relations.
>   Available at lutheranupress.org.

Over 50 real-life cases of interreligious engagement in ELCA ministry contexts are woven together with historical analysis, practical tips, and theological reflection. This book may be used in various educational settings (such as synod assemblies, convocations, theological conferences, rostered and lay leader gatherings, and congregational study groups).

Martin Luther: Visionary Reformer
>   By Scott H. Hendrix. Available at amazon.com.

Martin Luther was neither an unblemished saint nor a single-minded religious zealot, according to this provocative new biography. The author presents Luther as a man of his time: a highly educated scholar and teacher and a gifted yet flawed human being driven by an optimistic yet ultimately unrealized vision of "true religion."

October 31, 1517: Martin Luther and the Day that Changed the World
>   By Martin E. Marty. Available at amazon.com.

One of the world's preeminent scholars of religion offers a succinct meditation on the Ninety-five Theses, summing up its history, its influence, and its meaning for today.

Films and Videos

Martin Luther

To be broadcast on PBS in 2017.

A new documentary filmed in Europe with a large cast and crew. Luther scholar Dr. Erik Herrmann was on location in Poland to ensure accuracy. Sponsored by Thrivent Financial.

Rick Steves's Luther and the Reformation

To be broadcast on PBS in 2017.

A trip through the sites of Luther's life and Reformation guided by ELCA member Rick Steves.

From Conflict to Convergence

Available at ELCA500.org.

Dr. Timothy Wengert presented this special convocation, "From Conflict to Convergence," exploring the continued redevelopment of the relationship between the Lutheran church and other denominations and the Roman Catholic Church post-Reformation. The convocation was held Tuesday, October 6, 2015, a short time after Pope Francis left Philadelphia after the World Meeting of Families 2015.

Reformation Roots

Available from selectlearning.org.

Do you ever wonder why we have so many Christian denominations and if there is really much difference between them? The answers to these questions lie in the dramatic and turbulent times of the Reformation. This high-definition series brings to life the stories and struggles that still have an impact on us today. Each session is 20–30 minutes long and is accompanied by a study guide designed for 50–60 minutes of class time.

"We Must Plant the Church": The Story of Lutherans in America

Available from selectlearning.org.

When Lutherans came to America, they brought with them Martin Luther's belief that people of faith engage the big questions of the day. This DVD series on the history of Lutherans in America transports learners through four centuries of the planting of the Lutheran church in this new land. Henry Muhlenberg provided the title for this series. His motto was *Ecclesia Plantanda*: "We must plant the church."

Websites

www.elca500.org

This site lifts up the Evangelical Lutheran Church in America's Reformation observances and facilitates connections among ELCA partners, networks, and expressions. Find news and resources, explore upcoming events, and share your own ideas and activities.

www.2017.lutheranworld.org

Connect with Lutherans around the globe at the Lutheran World Federation's Reformation anniversary site under the theme "Liberated by God's Grace."

REFORMATION ANNIVERSARY COMMUNICATIONS GUIDE
A Resource for Working with Your Local Media

The Evangelical Lutheran Church in America (ELCA) is observing the 500th anniversary of the Reformation under the theme "Freed and renewed in Christ." The following resources and ideas are offered to assist ELCA congregations and communities of faith as they engage in communications about the anniversary both internally and with their broader communities.

Steps to Media Relations

The 500th anniversary of the Reformation is an opportunity for the Evangelical Lutheran Church in America to bear witness to the hope and joy we have through Jesus Christ. Many people will be asking about the significance of what happened 500 years ago when Martin Luther prepared and posted his 95 theses.

Connecting with the media in your community will create an opportunity to increase awareness of your congregation's plans to observe this significant milestone. It's also an opportunity to share with your community how your congregation serves its neighbors as Lutherans in today's world.

Luther's action started a dialogue that changed the way we receive and share the gospel, which continues today. This anniversary is an opportunity to communicate the Reformation's significance for faith and life in the twenty-first century and the freedom we have in Christ that liberates us to joyfully serve our neighbors.

All ELCA congregations are encouraged to plan and participate in activities that prepare for this milestone anniversary. These activities will allow us to give thanks for the word's power to free and renew all creation in Christ as well as provide an opportunity to emphasize the continuing work of reconciliation in the Christian church with our ecumenical partners.

Before engaging the media, you may want to consider these steps:

Build

Build upon current relations with your local media as we approach the 500th anniversary. Ultimately, the media will decide what is newsworthy, but it will be helpful to be prepared to engage with your community about who we are as Lutherans, how we are observing this significant milestone, and what it means for us today.

If you have not developed a relationship with your local print and broadcast media, the 500th anniversary is a great opportunity to do so. Your introduction should not necessarily focus on a single event. It should be about communicating your congregation's evangelical mission and witness in the community. How are your members making a difference in the world?

Designate

Designate someone in your congregation to be the media contact. This person will communicate specifics of the observance with the local media, send updated news releases, and make follow-up calls to media. This person will also help prepare two to three members or congregation staff for interviews.

The goal is to generate media interest about the 500th anniversary of the Reformation and your congregation's observance as part of a larger churchwide anniversary observed by millions of Lutherans around the world.

Prepare

Make use of the resources available to you.

Visit www.ELCA500.org, which hosts Reformation anniversary resources, news, and event highlights from local, national, and international ELCA partners in mission (including, but not limited to, synods, the churchwide organization, The Lutheran World Federation and Augsburg Fortress).

Prepare information for your congregation to learn more about the upcoming 500th anniversary on your congregation's internal and external communication channels.

NEWS RELEASES

Prepare a news release to share your congregation's observance plan with your local media. You may want to share a general 500th anniversary news release and then a specific observance news release about two weeks before your congregation's observance. You may use the news release template in the sourcebook digital files to get started.

Common themes for media interest may be an event you're planning with another congregation in the community, a project you're working on to observe the anniversary or engagement with your local ecumenical and interreligious sisters and brothers.

The ELCA's churchwide organization public relations team will also continue to write news releases on the anniversary, specifically in the fall of 2017, that congregations are able to share, which will include statements and quotes from leaders, such as Presiding Bishop Elizabeth Eaton. To see all current press releases, visit www.ELCA.org/News-and-Events.

INTERVIEWS

Choose two or three people from your congregation who feel comfortable speaking to the media and who are able to communicate your congregation's plans for the 500th anniversary observance. They should also have the ability to communicate your congregation's mission and witness as Lutherans.

Familiarize these people with the Reformation anniversary FAQ to assist with broad topics. Be able to answer the basic questions about your observance of the anniversary. The person being interviewed should be prepared to identify:

- Who: Who is participating in the observance? Who is invited?
- What: What will you do to observe this milestone?
- When: When is the anniversary and when is your observance?
- Where: Where will you host the observance?
- Why: Why is this milestone significant? Why is your congregation observing the way that you are?

Engage

Media outreach includes both traditional outlets—newspaper, radio and television—and social media platforms, such as Facebook, Twitter, and Pinterest, and other media tools your congregation uses.

Making information readily available creates a path for members and friends to learn about the 500th anniversary and your observance.

- Prepare your congregation's print and digital resources to reflect your upcoming plans and resources for the 500th. This will increase awareness and provide clarity.
- Create bulletin inserts and prepare temple talks to engage your congregation. By increasing awareness, you will make it easier for the media (and members) to engage with your plans.
- Consider how you will update your congregation's website, social media presence, and bulletin board to reflect plans and opportunities for involvement.

Remember that providing digital and print resources is helpful for not only current members but also the media and potential new members to learn about the ways our church is observing this significant milestone.

Once you're ready to engage the public, pitch your congregation's story to your local media. You may use the news release template in the sourcebook CD-ROM to get started.

Stay Connected

ELCA500.org is the digital information clearing house for ELCA Reformation anniversary information. You will find resources, events, connections to partners and networks, and more for you and your congregation to make use of as you prepare for your observance.

Social media

If your congregation has a Facebook page, Twitter handle, or other social media and you haven't yet started sharing information on the 500th anniversary on a local, national, or international level, you can begin sharing posts, news, and resources for your members surrounding the Reformation to spark interest.

Facebook

If you do not currently have a social media presence (and even if you do), you may direct media and your members to the ELCA's Facebook page designed to be an informational hub specific to Reformation anniversary news, resources, and events across the ELCA. **ELCA Reformation 500** is *a public page* open to all for information and shareable posts on resources, news, and events. Please feel free to use or "share" anything posted to support your social media strategy.

There is also an **ELCA Reformation 500** *closed facebook group* for conversation among other observance planners. Please join the conversation as we move forward into the 500th anniversary together.

You may also want to connect with your synod Facebook page to learn about what is going on at the synod level.

On Facebook, Instagram, and Twitter, use hashtag #ELCA500 to cluster your Reformation anniversary posts with other ELCA congregations!

Continue

Many synods also have 500th anniversary planning teams that may be able to assist your congregation. We encourage you to reach out to your synod office to learn more!

- Reach out to your synod for continued support and future Reformation anniversary opportunities.
- Continue to be in conversation with media through October of 2017.
- Support and empower members to learn more about Reformation anniversary-related projects. Prepare paths for engagement and provide connections to current paths for members to learn more about the global scope of this milestone.

Reformation Anniversary FAQ

Preparing to speak with a reporter includes anticipating the types of issues and concerns the reporter's audience may be interested in. Questions will vary according to the publication's or broadcast's audience and local or regional factors. The sample list of questions and responses below illustrate an approach that uses ordinary language as much as possible to focus on the central issue of God's grace in Christ and the relationships that emerge from a confidence in that grace. The list of sample questions and answers is also available on ELCA500.org/FAQ.

MARTIN LUTHER AND LUTHERANS TODAY

Who was Martin Luther?

Martin Luther was a Catholic monk and priest living in Wittenberg, Germany, in the early 1500s. When he began questioning the church teaching that was used to justify selling indulgences, a fierce controversy began over the church's teachings on forgiveness, grace, and faith; the content of preaching; and the church's ministry. Luther was eventually excommunicated from the church and outlawed by civil authorities, but his witness of God's forgiving mercy in Christ found many supporters.

What happened on October 31, 1517?

On this date Luther sent a letter to the Catholic archbishop of Mainz that urged renewed preaching of "the gospel and the love of Christ" instead of continued promotion of indulgences, which had "silenced" gospel preaching. He did not choose the day at random. Church representatives were actively marketing indulgences in a neighboring area, and the next day, All Saints Day, was a church festival associated with the church's teaching on merits, which was used to promote the selling of indulgences. He also enclosed a copy of his 95 theses, which were also likely posted on the door of the Castle Church in Wittenberg that same day.

Why is this still relevant today?

All of us continue to live in a culture where judgment, guilt, and shame are everyday experiences and where bullying words, abusive actions, and shaming political discourse permeate our public and private lives. The indulgences controversy may be a relic of the past, but the healing and reconciling message of God's mercy and forgiveness in Christ that Luther and others served is still needed—and still surprisingly contested.

Who are ELCA Lutherans today? What is your teaching and practice?

Whenever ELCA Lutherans gather and are asked for one word to describe who they are, overwhelmingly the answer is "grace." Martin Luther described grace as "God's favor or good will toward us" in Jesus Christ. This liberating experience of who God is for humankind is the heart of Lutheran teaching and practice as Lutherans live and serve in a wide range of contexts in the United States and globally.

Why do you have the word "evangelical" in your name? What does that mean?

"Evangelical" combines two Greek words that mean message and good (news). Martin Luther and others in the sixteenth century called themselves "evangelicals" because they were committed to proclaiming and serving the message of good news in Jesus Christ—that is, the message of God's forgiving mercy and compassion. The ELCA continues to use this name for the same reason. (A later group of Christians in England and the United States who emphasized preaching and moral conversion—"Evangelicalism"—also came to be called "evangelicals," and this label is often used today in popular media to identify a wide range of politically active, conservative American Christians.)

LUTHERANS, OTHER CHRISTIANS, AND OTHER FAITHS

What do Lutherans say about Luther's writings about the Jews?

Martin Luther's writings, especially from his last years, include statements composed of a handful of writings that were extreme in their judgments against the Jewish people and their religious practices, even by the standards of his time. The reasons for these writings and their effects on others have been debated, but the condemnations and endorsements of violence in these writings are indefensible. Since the Holocaust, Lutheran church bodies, including the ELCA and The Lutheran World Federation, have acknowledged the great harm done by these writings, repudiated their judgments, and committed to a more responsible relationship with Jewish people.

What is the relationship between Lutherans and the Roman Catholic Church today?
In the last 50 years Lutherans and Catholics have been engaged in dialogues both nationally and globally that have led to a remarkable series of agreements on church teaching and practice. The "Joint Declaration on the Doctrine of Justification" (1999) was a milestone in Lutheran–Catholic relations, and "Declaration on the Way" (2015) brings together 32 consensus statements on church, ministry, and eucharist from conversations that still continue. Another statement, "From Conflict to Communion," helped shape the Common Prayer liturgy which Pope Francis will celebrate with Lutheran leaders on October 31, 2016.

What do Lutherans say about Muslims?
In recent years the ELCA and The Lutheran World Federation have been talking *with* Muslims, both listening and speaking respectfully in gatherings committed to mutual understanding and improved relationships. Both nationally and globally, Lutheran agencies have collaborated with Muslim counterparts in projects that address humanitarian needs. In these activities Lutherans seek to know and understand their Muslim neighbors better so that they can speak more graciously and responsibly in conversations too often filled with inflammatory and hateful speech.

THE ELCA AND THE 500TH ANNIVERSARY

Where does the theme "Freed and Renewed in Christ" come from?
In "The Freedom of a Christian" (1520) Martin Luther famously wrote, "A Christian is lord of all, completely free of everything; a Christian is a servant, completely attentive to the needs of all." The ELCA's theme expresses this message of the Christian faith's freedom and a renewed life of service to others in Jesus Christ.

Marcus Kunz and Amanda Lauer

PERMISSION GUIDELINES FOR IMAGE USE

BULLETIN INSERTS

The bulletin inserts on pages 133–156 of this Sourcebook are also available as full color PDF files on the CD-ROM bound with this book. Unaltered inserts may be reproduced and distributed in print or electronically by the purchaser of this volume for onetime, non-sale use, provided copies are for local use only and the printed copyright notice appears.

Page 133: Drawing of Wittenberg in 1536 from the travel album of Count Palatine Ottheinrich. Pen and ink, watercolor. University of Würzburg. www.ottheinrich.info.

Page 134: *Martin Luther* (1526) by Lucas Cranach the Elder (1472–1553). Oil on oak. Private collection, Hamburg.

Page 135: *Die Wartburg* by Friedrich von Sydow from *Thüringen und der Harz mit ihren Merkwürdigkeiten, Volkssagen und Legenden*, vol. 2 (Sondershausen, 1839). Lithograph. British Library/Mechanical Curator collection.

Page 136: Title woodcut for the 1541 version of Martin Luther's German Bible by Lucas Cranach the Younger (1515–1586).

Page 137: Image © Augsburg Fortress, 2016.

Page 138: Woodcut of Christ teaching the disciples the Lord's Prayer by Hans Brosamer (1495–1554) from the 1550 Frankfurt edition of the *Small Catechism of Martin Luther*. Woodcut and letterpress. The British Museum.

Page 139: *Augsburg Confession 1530* by Karl Remshard (1678–1735) from the Elector Bible, Nürnburg, 1720. Engraving.

Page 140: Philipp Melanchthon (1532) by Lucas Cranach the Elder (1472–1553). Oil on beech wood. Historisches Museum Regensburg.

Page 141: Portrait Medal of Argula von Grumbach (c. 1520) by Hans Schwarz (1492–c. 1532). Cast lead. Germanisches Nationalmuseum, Nürnburg

Page 142: *Katharina von Bora* (c. 1526) by Lucas Cranach the Elder (1472–1553). Oil on oak. Private collection, Hamburg.

Page 143: Statue of the brothers Olavus and Laurentius Petri by Nils A. G. Sjögren (1894–1952) at Olaus Petri Church, Örebro, Sweden. Photo © Edaen. Licensed under the Creative Commons Attribution 3.0 Unported license.

Page 144: *Mikael Agricola* by Albert Edelfelt (1854–1905). Finnish.

Page 145: Portrait of Henry Melchior Muhlenberg (c. 1825–1850). After Jacob Eichholtz (1776–1842). Oil on canvas. Preservation Society of Newport County, Newport, Rhode Island.

Page 146: Photo © Evangelical Lutheran Church in America. Used by permission.

Page 147: Frederick Lutheran Church, Charlotte Amalie, St. Thomas, Virgin Islands. Photo © Steve Heap/Shutterstock.com. Used by permission.

Page 148: Steps Beach in Rincon, Puerto Rico. Photo © Stacy Hall. Used by permission.

Page 149: "Immigrants Landing at Ellis Island" (c. 1900) by Brown Brothers, New York, NY. National Archives and Records Administration, Records of the Public Health Service, 1912–1968.

Page 150: Worship, Regional Workshop on Gender Justice, Hermeneutics, and Development, Johannesburg, South Africa, November 2014. Photo © 2014 Lutheran World Federation/E. Neuenfeldt. Permission requested.

Page 151: Portrait of Theodor Fliedner (1800–1864). Social welfare stamp series, 1952. Intaglio. Deutsche Bundespost, Germany.

Page 152: Portrait of Elisabeth Fedde (c. 1880). Artist unknown. Norwegian-American Historical Association.

Page 153: *Luther Making Music in the Circle of His Family* (c. 1875) by Gustav Spangenberg (1828–1891).

Page 154: Photo © Ike Sturm. Used by permission.

Page 155: Portrait of Hans Nielsen Hauge (c. 1800). Artist unknown. Copenhagen.

CD-ROM-ONLY IMAGES FOR "THE CHURCH'S JOURNEY IN ART AND SONG"

Electronic files of the artwork used in the ELCA's 2015 Worship Jubilee, "Called to Be a Living Voice," are available on the CD-ROM bound with this book. Permission is granted to purchasers of the Reformation 500 Sourcebook *for onetime or one-season use as unaltered projected content for worship or study concerning the 500th anniversary of the Reformation. They may not be distributed, sold, or included in collections or publications. They may not be used in print publications (for example, bulletins, newsletters, ads) or online (for example, blogs, church websites) without additional permission from the copyright holder. Information to assist you in securing additional permission for such uses is included with each image listed below.*

The Church's Journey in Art and Song title slide by Clayton Faulkner. Image © Pixabay.com.
No additional permission required.

The Blind Singer (El cantor ciego) (1824–1828) by Francisco de Goya y Lucientes (1746–1828). Etching, aquatint, drypoint, and burin on laid paper. Copyright © The Metropolitan Museum of Art/Art Resource, NY. Used by permission.
Permission requests: www.artres.com.

The Denial of Saint Peter (c. 1610) by Michelangelo Merisi da Caravaggio (1573–1610). Oil on canvas. Copyright © The Metropolitan Museum of Art/Art Resource, NY. Used by permission.
Permission requests: www.artres.com.

Women at the Tomb of Christ (3rd cent.). Unknown Syrian wall painting in the *domus ecclesiae* (an early house church) in Dura-Europos, a Hellenistic, Parthian, and Roman border city built near the Euphrates river, now located in present-day Syria.
No additional permission required.

The Crucifixion; Calvary (1502) by Lucas Cranach the Elder (1472–1553). Woodcut. Copyright © The Metropolitan Museum of Art/Art Resource, NY. Used by permission.
Permission requests: www.artres.com.

A Mighty Fortress by Mary Button. Watercolor. Copyright © 2015 Mary Button. Used by permission.
Permission requests: marybethbutton@gmail.com.

Messiah by He Qi. Copyright © 2014 He Qi. All rights reserved. Used by permission.
Permission requests: www.heqiart.com.

Simon of Cyrene Helps Jesus Carry the Cross by Mary Button. Watercolor. Copyright © 2014 Mary Button. Used by permission.
Permission requests: marybethbutton@gmail.com.

Wisdom. Illuminated manuscript (c. 1170), Hildesheim, Germany. Tempera colors, gold leaf, silver leaf, and ink on parchment. J. Paul Getty Museum, Los Angeles, CA.
No additional permission required. www.getty.edu/about/opencontent.html.